Daily Skill Builders:
Reading
Grades 5–6

By
PATRICIA McFADDEN

COPYRIGHT © 2007 Mark Twain Media, Inc.

ISBN 978-1-58037-413-2

Printing No. CD-404072

Mark Twain Media, Inc., Publishers
Distributed by Carson-Dellosa Publishing Company, Inc.

Table of Contents

Table of Contents (cont.)

Introduction to the Teacher

Both the No Child Left Behind Act and standardized testing require students to meet certain proficiency standards. The *Daily Skill Builders* in this book have been written with both of these sets of requirements in mind. (See the following website for National ELA Standards as supported by NCTE and IRA <http://www.ncte.org/about/over/standards/110846.htm>). Standards matrixes for selected states are provided on pages 1–3. These give teachers the specific reading, writing, and language standards that are covered by each activity in this book.

The exercises in this book will give students daily practice in such important reading skills as identifying the author's purpose, making inferences, remembering details, and looking for context clues. Fourteen specific reading skills in all are addressed using a variety of applications.

In addition, the exercises are labeled by skill and grouped by grade-appropriate topic. This way, teachers may quickly and conveniently access all the drills for a specific skill focus or include a comprehensive set of drills in a study unit for a particular topic.

We hope you and your students find these exercises both useful and engaging. Reading and writing are the tools upon which all other academic endeavors, including high achievement on tests, ultimately rely. These *Daily Skill Builders* are designed to help your students hone their literacy tools to razor sharpness.

In short, use these *Daily Skill Builders* any and every way you can to make the most of all the tools packed inside. Expect your students' reading, writing, and spelling skills to grow throughout year!

California Standards Matrix for Grades 5–6

LANGUAGE ARTS STANDARDS	ACTIVITIES
READING	
Use word, sentence, and paragraph clues to determine meaning of unknown words.	3, 17, 20, 31, 45, 59, 73, 87, 101, 115, 118, 129, 143, 146, 157, 160
Understand how text features (e.g., format, graphics, sequence, diagrams, illustrations, charts, maps) make information accessible and usable.	2, 6, 13, 16, 27, 41, 44, 48, 58, 72, 86, 104, 128, 142, 153, 167
Analyze text that uses an organizational pattern (e.g., sequential or chronological order, compare and contrast).	2, 4, 9, 13, 16, 18, 23, 27, 30, 32, 37, 41, 44, 46, 51, 55, 58, 60, 65, 69, 72, 74, 83, 86, 88, 93, 97, 100, 102, 104, 107, 111, 114, 116, 125, 128, 130, 135, 139, 142, 144, 149, 153, 156, 158, 163, 167
Make, modify, and confirm inferences, conclusions, or generalizations about text and support them with textual evidence and prior knowledge.	1, 7, 10, 12, 14, 15, 21, 24, 26, 28, 29, 34, 35, 38, 40, 42, 43, 49, 52, 54, 56, 57, 63, 66, 68, 70, 71, 77, 80, 82, 84, 85, 91, 94, 96, 98, 99, 105, 108, 110, 112, 113, 119, 122, 124, 126, 127, 132, 133, 136, 138, 140, 141, 147, 150, 152, 154, 155, 161, 164, 166, 168
Distinguish facts, supported inferences, and opinions in text.	8, 22, 36, 50, 64, 78, 92, 106, 120, 134, 148, 162
Connect and clarify main ideas by identifying their relationships to related topics.	7, 23, 30, 31, 35, 47, 119
Define how tone or meaning is conveyed in poetry through word choice, figurative language, sentence structure, line length, punctuation, rhythm, repetition, and rhyme.	5, 19, 33, 47, 61, 75, 103, 117, 131, 145, 159
Analyze characters, including their traits, motivations, conflicts, points of view, relationships, and changes they undergo.	11, 14, 25, 28, 53, 56, 67, 70, 81, 84, 95, 98, 109, 112, 123, 126, 137, 140, 151, 154, 165, 168
WRITING	
Write narratives that establish a plot, point of view, setting, conflict, and use narrative devices (e.g., dialogue, suspense).	24, 26, 79, 93
Write responses to literature that demonstrate an understanding of a literary work, support judgments through references to the text and to prior knowledge, and develop interpretations.	37, 38, 92
LANGUAGE CONVENTIONS	
Use simple, compound, and compound-complex sentences; use effective coordination and subordination of ideas to express complete thoughts.	12, 14, 24, 26, 37, 38, 40, 79, 82, 93
Use correct capitalization.	12, 14, 24, 26, 40, 79, 82, 93
Spell roots, affixes, contractions, and syllable constructions correctly.	12, 14, 24, 26, 40, 79, 82, 93

Florida Standards Matrix for Grades 5–6

LANGUAGE ARTS STANDARDS	
READING	
Use a variety of strategies to monitor texts (e.g., rereading, self-correcting, summarizing, checking other sources, using context and word structure clues).	3, 9, 12, 14, 17, 20, 28, 31, 37, 40, 41, 42, 45, 51, 54, 56, 59, 65, 70, 73, 82, 84, 87, 96, 98, 101, 107, 110, 112, 115, 121, 129, 135, 140, 143, 149, 152, 154, 157, 163, 168
Understand explicit and implicit ideas and information in texts (e.g., main idea, inferences, relevant supporting details, fact vs. opinion, generalizations, conclusions).	6, 7, 8, 11, 12, 14, 21, 22, 25, 26, 28, 34, 35, 36, 39, 42, 48, 49, 50, 53, 54, 56, 62, 63, 64, 67, 68, 70, 76, 77, 78, 81, 82, 84, 90, 91, 92, 95, 98, 104, 105, 106, 109, 110, 112, 118, 119, 120, 121, 122, 123, 124, 125, 126, 132, 133, 134, 137, 138, 140, 146, 147, 148, 149, 152, 154, 160, 161, 162, 165, 166, 168
Describe author's purpose and how an author's perspective influences the text.	1, 15, 29, 43, 57, 71, 85, 99, 113, 127, 141, 155
Analyze ways writers organize and present ideas (e.g., comparison–contrast, cause–effect, chronology).	2, 4, 13, 16, 18, 23, 27, 30, 32, 41, 44, 46, 55, 58, 60, 69, 72, 74, 83, 86, 88, 97, 100, 102, 104, 111, 114, 116, 125, 128, 130, 139, 142, 144, 153, 156, 158, 167
Read from and understand the distinguishing features of literary texts (e.g., historical fiction, drama, poetry, autobiography, myths, folktales).	7, 23, 30, 31, 32, 33, 35, 37, 38, 40, 41, 43, 47, 63, 77, 93, 103, 105, 119, 131, 146, 147
Read from and understand the distinguishing features of nonfiction texts (e.g., textbooks, scientific studies, magazines, newspapers).	49, 86, 88, 90, 91, 130, 132
Make inferences and draw conclusions regarding story elements (e.g., the characters' traits and actions, plot development, setting, point of view).	5, 10, 24, 33, 38, 47, 52, 61, 66, 75, 80, 89, 94, 103, 108, 117, 136, 145, 150, 159
Respond to literature by explaining how the motives of the characters and the causes of events compare with those of own life.	19, 89
WRITING	
Use a variety of sentence structures to reinforce ideas.	12, 23, 24, 26, 37, 38, 40, 79, 82, 93
Use conventions of punctuation and capitalization.	12, 24, 26, 37, 38, 40, 79, 82, 93
Use various parts of speech correctly in writing (e.g., subject-verb agreement, noun and verb forms, objective and subjective case pronouns, correct form of adjectives and adverbs).	12, 24, 26, 37, 38, 40, 79, 82, 93
Write for a variety of occasions, audiences, and purposes (e.g., letters to invite or thank, stories or poems to entertain, information to record, notes and summaries reflecting comprehension).	12, 24, 26, 37, 38, 40, 79, 82, 93

Texas Standards Matrix for Grades 5–6

LANGUAGE ARTS STANDARDS	ACTIVITIES
READING	
Apply knowledge of letter-sound correspondences, structural analysis, and context to recognize words and identify root words with affixes.	3, 17, 20, 31, 34, 45, 59, 62, 73, 87, 101, 115, 129, 143, 157
Establish purposes for reading, such as to be informed, to follow directions, to be entertained, to solve problems, and to discover models for own writing.	1, 9, 15, 23 ,29, 37, 43, 51, 57, 62, 65, 71, 85, 93, 99, 107, 113, 121, 127, 135, 141, 149, 155, 163
Follow strategies for comprehension while reading, such as rereading, using reference aids, searching for clues, and asking questions.	12, 26, 40, 54, 68, 82, 90, 96, 110, 112, 124, 138, 152, 166
Determine a text's main ideas and how those ideas are supported with details.	11, 25, 39, 53, 67, 81, 95, 109, 123, 137, 151, 165
Draw inferences such as conclusions or generalizations and support them with text evidence and experience.	10, 21, 24, 38, 52, 66, 80, 94, 108, 122, 136, 150, 164
Paraphrase and summarize text to recall, inform, and organize ideas.	14, 28, 42, 56, 70, 84, 112, 140, 154, 168
Distinguish fact and opinion in various texts.	8, 22, 36, 50, 64, 78, 92, 106, 120, 134, 148, 162
Represent text information in different ways, such as in outlines, timelines, and graphic organizers.	6, 48, 76, 90, 104, 160
LITERARY RESPONSE AND CONCEPTS	
Understand literary forms by distinguishing among types of texts as stories, poems, myths, fables, tall tales, limericks, plays, informational texts, biographies, and autobiographies.	7, 21, 23, 31, 32, 33, 34, 35, 37, 38, 40, 41, 43, 47, 49, 63, 77, 80, 91, 93, 104, 105, 117, 118, 119, 130, 131, 132, 146
Analyze characters, including their traits, motivations, conflicts, points of view, relationships, and changes they undergo.	5, 19, 33, 47, 61, 75, 89, 103, 117, 131, 145, 159
Analyze ways authors organize and present ideas such as through cause/effect, compare/contrast, or chronologically.	2, 4, 7, 13, 16, 18, 27, 30, 32, 41, 44, 46, 55, 58, 60, 69, 72, 74, 77, 83, 86, 88, 100, 102, 105, 111, 114, 116, 125, 128, 130, 133, 139, 142, 144, 147, 153, 156, 158, 161, 167
Use and interpret text organizers and graphic sources to locate information.	6, 13, 27, 48, 69, 128
WRITING	
Write for a variety of audiences and purposes, such as to express, to influence, to inform, to entertain, to record, to problem solve, and to reflect.	12, 26, 37, 38, 40, 79, 82, 93
Compose original texts, applying the conventions of written language, such as capitalization, punctuation, and penmanship, to communicate clearly.	12, 26, 37, 38, 40, 79, 82, 93
Write with accurate spelling of roots, inflections, affixes, and syllable constructions.	12, 26, 37, 38, 40, 79, 82, 93
Write in complete sentences, varying the types such as compound and complex to match meanings and purposes.	12, 26, 37, 38, 40, 79, 82, 93

Oceans

 **ACTIVITY 1** **Author's Purpose**

Name:_____

Date:_____

Read the following paragraphs. Decide if the author's purpose is to entertain, inform, or persuade. Then put a plus (+) next to the answer.

1. "Shark!" The cry sends terror through the hearts of all. These denizens of the deep are the stuff of nightmares. They are silent and deadly with rows and rows of razor-sharp teeth that can rip a person apart in a matter of seconds, and they are always hungry. No place that is next to the ocean is entirely safe. Sharks have been known to attack in as little as three or four feet of water. So, next time you're at the beach, keep a sharp eye out. And, if anyone yells, "Shark!" head for shore. It might be a joke, but then again ... it might not.

   _____ entertain   _____ inform   _____ persuade

2. Sharks are believed to be the first animal to develop teeth. Shark teeth are arranged in rows, with each row of teeth being a bit smaller than the one in front. Some sharks have five,  some as many as twenty, rows of teeth. If a shark loses a tooth, the one behind it moves up to replace it within twenty-four hours. A shark's mouth is like a tooth conveyor belt with old teeth being replaced by new ones throughout the shark's life. Some sharks, such as dog sharks, have small, blunt teeth. Others, like tiger sharks and great white sharks, have razor-sharp teeth.

   _____ entertain   _____ inform   _____ persuade

ACTIVITY 2 **Compare and Contrast**

Name:_____

Date:_____

Read the following, and then fill in the Venn diagram below.

Both squid and octopi (the plural of octopus) are **cephalopods**. Both have tentacles. Both come in many sizes. Squid, however, have bullet-shaped heads and ten tentacles. Octopi have rounded heads and eight tentacles. Both squid and octopi have suckers on their tentacles that they use to catch prey. Both have a bony beak. Both squid and octopi lay eggs. An octopus mother, however, keeps watch over her eggs. A squid mother does not. Some octopi can measure 50 feet from their head to the ends of their tentacles. Squid get even larger. Scientists think there may be giant squid in the deep ocean that are 200 feet long.

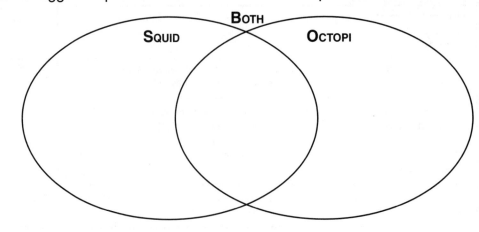

Oceans (cont.)

ACTIVITY 3 **Context Clues**

Name:_____

Date:_____

Use context clues to help you choose the correct word for each sentence below.

crust   **irregularity**   **approximately**   **submerged**

1. _____ three-fourths of the earth is covered in water to an average depth of more than two miles. If the earth's _____ was smooth, it would be _____ in about 8,000 feet of water. It is the _____ of the earth's surface that makes continents possible.

concerning   **millennia**   **dwells**   **perfectly**

2. Five-sixths of all life on Earth _____ in the sunlit upper reaches of the ocean. Each of the hundreds of thousands of species of sea creatures is _____ suited to its habitat. Though humans have explored the oceans for _____, there are still many mysteries _____ the ocean and its creatures that we have yet to solve.

ACTIVITY 4 **Cause and Effect**

Name:_____

Date:_____

Read the paragraph below. Complete the charts by filling in the missing cause or effect.

Electric eels are living batteries. Their bodies are about 75% electricity-generating tissue. All living creatures emit at least some electricity, which is how an eel hunts its prey. The eel's body is covered with pits. These pits are electrical sensors. When an electric eel senses another energy field nearby, it gives off a burst of electricity that stuns or kills its prey. A really big electrical eel can give off as much as 600 volts of electricity, which is enough to seriously injure or kill a human.

Cause	**Effect**
1. Electric eel bodies are 75% electricity-generating tissue.	_____
2. _____	This is how an eel hunts its prey.
3. The eel's body is covered with pits.	_____
4. _____	The eel gives off a burst of electricity.
5. _____	This is enough to injure or kill a human.

5

Oceans (cont.)

ACTIVITY 5 Character Analysis

Name:_____

Date:_____

Read the paragraph, and then circle the character traits below that you think best describe Jacques Cousteau.

Jacques Cousteau was a well-known oceanographer. His movies about the sea and its inhabitants have helped people understand the importance of oceans. Cousteau was born in 1910. He liked to invent things and was fascinated by the sea. He served in the French Navy during World War II, where he learned to be a deep-sea diver. After that, his dream was to own his own ocean research vessel. He bought the *Calypso* in 1950, fitted it out, and spent the rest of his life sailing around the world learning about marine life and making movies about the sea. All his life, he spoke for peace and for cooperation in caring for the world's oceans and seas.

lazy	impatient	brave	cowardly	curious
patient	caring	foolish	intelligent	determined

ACTIVITY 6 Details

Name:_____

Date:_____

Read the selection, and then write the parts of the water cycle on the diagram below.

Rain falls on a mountaintop and begins to travel downstream. At first, it is a rivulet. Then, it joins with other rivulets to become a small stream that flows into a larger stream. The larger stream empties into a river. The river connects to a larger river. The big river ends in a delta and empties into a bay or a gulf, which widens into a sea and eventually becomes an ocean. The water in the ocean evaporates, condenses to form clouds, and travels across the land. Eventually, it falls as precipitation (rain or snow) and makes the journey back to the ocean again. As you can see, the waters of the earth are all connected.

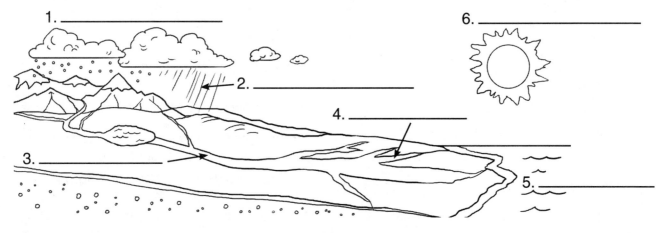

1. _____

6. _____

2. _____

4. _____

3. _____

5. _____

Oceans (cont.)

ACTIVITY 7 **Drawing Conclusions**

Name: _____

Date: _____

Read the following stanzas from a famous poem, and then answer the questions below.

Seal Lullaby by Rudyard Kipling

Oh! hush thee, my baby, the night is behind us,
And black are the waters that sparkle so green.
The moon, o'er the combers, looks downward to find us
At rest in the hollows that rustle between.
Where billow meets billow, there soft be thy pillow;
Ah, weary wee flipperling, curl at thy ease!
The storm shall not wake thee,
In the arms of the slow-swinging seas.

1. Who is the "flipperling" in line 6? _____

2. The words "billows" and "combers" both refer to what?

   a. ocean waves   b. beach scavengers   c. sails

3. What does the line "Black are the waters that sparkle so green" mean?

   _____

   _____

ACTIVITY 8 **Fact and Opinion**

Name: _____

Date: _____

A fact can be proved. An opinion is what you believe or think. Read the sentences below. Put "F" by the facts and "O" by the opinions.

_____ 1. I simply adore sailing on the ocean.

_____ 2. It takes a lot of skill and practice to handle a sailboat.

_____ 3. Schooners are large sailing ships with complicated rigging.

_____ 4. Everyone should go on a sea voyage at least once in their life.

_____ 5. It sometimes took whaling ships years to get to their destination.

_____ 6. English sailors were called "limeys" because they took lime juice with them to prevent scurvy.

_____ 7. I think it would be terrible to develop scurvy and lose all your teeth.

Oceans (cont.)

ACTIVITY 9   **Following Directions**   Name:_____

Date:_____

Follow the directions below to make an origami fish.
1. Use origami paper or cut a 3- or 4-inch square of wrapping paper.
2. With printed side facing up, fold in half along center. (a)
3. Unfold and, with printed side down, fold from corner to corner both ways. (b)
4. With printed side down, fold along creases to make a "tent." (c)
5. Make accordion pleats on each side for fins. (d)
6. Turn over and make smaller accordion pleats for tail. (e)
7. Draw eyes, mouth, and gills to complete. (f)

a.   b. 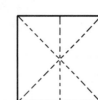 c.  d.   e.   f.

Bonus Activity: Make several origami fish of different sizes and colors. Hang them from the ceiling or use them to make a mobile.

ACTIVITY 10   **Inference**   Name:_____

Date:_____

Read the selection below, and then answer the questions below.

"Surf's up!" shouted Kanunu. He grabbed his board and ran down to the edge of the water, diving in and paddling out far enough to catch a really big wave.

"Look out!" Makani pointed to a dorsal fin sticking out of the water that was following close behind Kanunu. "Oh, never mind," she added as a sleek, gray body shot out of the water, turned a somersault, and dived back with a "chi-chi-chi" sound.

Makani was soon out with Kanunu, racing and laughing as they caught wave after perfect wave. A whole pod of finny friends swam around them. Puffy white clouds floated high above the palm trees on the shore. It was a beautiful day in paradise, and the two friends were making the most of it.

1. Where did this story take place?_____
2. How can you tell?_____
3. What are Kanunu and Makani doing?_____
4. Why was Makani frightened when she saw a fin?_____
5. To what did the fin belong?_____
6. How do you know?_____

Oceans (cont.)

ACTIVITY 11 Main Idea

Name:_____

Date:_____

Read the paragraph below, and then put a plus (+) next to the main idea.

A new kind of ocean exploration is possible because of Global Positioning System (GPS) technology. Before GPS, it was hard for divers to return to an exact spot on the ocean floor. Therefore, they would waste a lot of time hunting for things they'd already found. Now, they use a line attached to a float with a GPS transmitter and are able to return to the same spot, time after time. This technology also makes it possible to accurately map underwater cities, sunken fleets, and other deep-sea discoveries that shouldn't be moved. GPS has revolutionized the way underwater explorers and treasure hunters operate.

_____ 1. Many underwater discoveries shouldn't be moved.

_____ 2. Global Positioning System technology has changed how underwater exploration is done.

_____ 3. It's hard for divers to return to an exact spot under the sea.

ACTIVITY 12 Predicting Outcomes

Name:_____

Date:_____

Read the paragraph, and then finish the story of the baby sea turtle. Use your own paper if you need more room.

The baby sea turtle fought her way out of her shell. Scrambling over her brothers and sisters, she headed toward the scent of salt water. Sea birds swooped down, eager for an easy lunch. But she was lucky. No hungry gull grabbed her before she could get into the surf. In the end, only she and about two dozen of her hundred siblings made it into the water. Climbing on a clump of seaweed, the baby turtle hitched a ride on the warm Gulf Current. The seaweed was boat and dinner, all in one. The turtle's journey, across the Atlantic and back, had just begun.

Approximately one out of one hundred sea turtles survives to return to the beach where it was hatched to lay more eggs. Was this the lucky one, or not? _____

_____

_____

_____

_____

_____

Oceans (cont.)

ACTIVITY 13 **Sequencing**

Name:_____

Date:_____

Read the following paragraph, and then fill in the blanks on the flowchart below.

    The life cycle of a seahorse is very odd. After a male and female seahorse mate, the female deposits her eggs in a special pouch on the male seahorse's belly. The mother leaves, and the father seahorse becomes an incubator for the eggs. After the eggs hatch, the little seahorses stay close to their father. If danger threatens, he scoops them into his mouth to keep them safe. Once the babies are too big to fit in the father seahorse's mouth, he leaves them and goes off to find another mate to start the whole cycle again.

FLOWCHART FOR THE SEAHORSE LIFE CYCLE

1. After they mate, a female seahorse puts her eggs in a _____ on the male's belly.	2. The mother seahorse leaves, and the father seahorse becomes an _____.	3. After the eggs hatch, the little seahorses stay close to _____.
6. The father seahorse finds another mate and the _____ begins again.	5. Once the babies no longer fit in his mouth, the father seahorse _____.	4. If danger threatens, the father seahorse scoops them into his _____.

ACTIVITY 14 **Summarizing**

Name:_____

Date:_____

Read the paragraph, and then write a summarizing sentence.

    The ocean is divided into three zones, which are based on how far down sunlight can reach. Approximately the first 450 feet is the **Sunlit Zone**. Most marine life lives in this zone. In shallow seas, this is the only zone. In the open ocean, it is the upper reaches of the water. The **Twilight Zone**, from 450 to 3,300 feet down, gets some light. There are still quite a few animals at this depth, but no plants. Below 3,300 feet is the **Midnight Zone**, or **abyss**. No sunlight ever reaches this deep. However, there is still life here—strange fish with glowing bobbles or lighted spots along their bellies, giant squid, and tiny crustaceans.

Write a summarizing sentence. _____

_____

_____

_____

Japan and China

ACTIVITY 15   **Author's Purpose**

Name: _____

Date: _____

Read the following paragraphs. Decide if the author's purpose is to entertain, inform, or persuade. Then put a plus (+) next to the answer.

1. Many aspects of Japanese pop culture have found their way into other countries. This is because Japan is the source for many of the best computer games that have been developed in the past few years. They also export graphic novels, called *manga*, and animated films, or *anime*, both of which have many devoted fans the world over.

_____ entertain   _____ inform   _____ persuade

2. Rita loved to watch *anime* films. There was something about those funny, big-eyed characters that she found irresistible. Sometimes, she wished that she was an *anime* character, herself. *Kiki*, maybe, with her flying broomstick, or the sisters who rode in the cat bus with Totoro, or the girl in *Spirited Away* who had such interesting adventures. She wished she was anyone but quiet little Rita whom nobody ever noticed.

_____ entertain   _____ inform   _____ persuade

- -

ACTIVITY 16   **Compare and Contrast**

Name: _____

Date: _____

Read the following, and then fill in the Venn diagram below.

Japan is a series of islands off the east coast of Asia. China is a huge country on the same continent. Culturally, they have many similarities. In China, many people practice Buddhism, Taoism, and Confucianism. In Japan, many people practice Buddhism also, but their type of Buddhism is known as Zen. Many Japanese also follow the Shinto religion. Both China and Japan produce beautiful silk cloth. Both have pictographic writing. In China, there are around a billion people. In Japan, there are only about 150 million people. In terms of people per square mile, though, both their population densities are about the same.

Ways Japan and China Are Alike	Ways Japan and China Are Different	
	Japan	China
_____	_____	_____
_____	_____	_____
_____	_____	_____
_____	_____	_____
_____	_____	_____

Japan and China (cont.)

ACTIVITY 17 **Context Clues**

Name:_____

Date:_____

Choose a word or phrase from the Word Bank to replace the word in boldface in each sentence. Look for context clues to help you choose the right word.

WORD BANK					
about	required	specific	sources	made	native

1. Many Japanese words have Chinese **derivations**. _____

2. For writing foreign words, a **specialized** alphabet called *katekane* is used.

   _____

3. *Ainu*, spoken by the original, **indigenous** people of Japan is seldom heard.

   _____

4. **Approximately** 99% of the population speaks Japanese as their first language.

   _____

5. English is a **compulsory** course in most Japanese schools. _____

6. Both Chinese and Japanese writing are **composed** of pictographs.

   _____

- -

ACTIVITY 18 **Cause and Effect**

Name:_____

Date:_____

Read the paragraph below. Fill in the blanks for the missing cause or effect.

Because of World War II, much of Japan was in ruins in the late 1940s. Centuries of tradition and art were nearly gone. The Japanese wanted to do something to preserve what was left of their cultural heritage. In 1950, the government passed the Cultural Properties Protection Law. As part of this law, people who are thought to be masters of their craft are called "Bearers of Important Intangible Cultural Assets." There have been more than 100 of these named so far. They are popularly known as "Living National Treasures." Whenever a Living National Treasure is named, his or her art form gets a lot of attention and is more likely to continue.

1. _____ Japan was in bad shape.

2. Ancient traditions were being lost. _____

3. In 1950, the CPPL was enacted. _____

4. Some people are considered masters

   of an art. _____

5. _____ his or her artform is more likely to continue.

Japan and China (cont.)

ACTIVITY 19 **Character Analysis**

Name:_____

Date:_____

One of Japan's Living National Treasures, Yoshida Minsuke, is a *Bunraku* puppet master. It takes three people to operate a *Bunraku* puppet. Yoshida spent ten years moving only the legs of puppets. Then, he spent fifteen years operating only the left hands. At last, he became a master and now operates the right hand and heads of the puppets. *Bunraku* puppeteers have to cooperate to get the puppets to move just right.

1. Think of four words to describe Yoshida Minsuke's character. _____

    _____ _____ _____

2. Give an example of something you've done that shows a character trait you have that would

    be useful if you were a *Bunraku* puppeteer. _____

    _____

    _____

ACTIVITY 20 **Details**

Name:_____

Date:_____

Using the information in the following paragraph, answer the questions below.

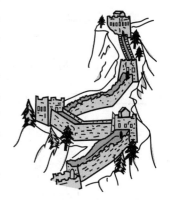

For fourteen hundred years, from the third century to the beginning of the seventeenth century A.D., the Chinese people worked on building their Great Wall. The Wall stretches all the way across the northern border of the country. It is nearly 4,000 miles long and separates China from modern-day Manchuria and Mongolia. In medieval times, it was named as one of the Seven Wonders of the World. The Great Wall of China is said to be the only manmade structure visible from space. This, however, isn't true. For one thing, it's not often visible because of cloud cover in the area. For another, there are other structures that, according to astronauts, are also visible. Nonetheless, it is a thrilling sight that draws many tourists every year.

1. It took _____ years to build the Great Wall of China.
2. The Great Wall is nearly _____ miles long.
3. The Great Wall stretches across the _____ border of China.
4. Today, the Great Wall is mainly useful as a _____ attraction.
5. The Great Wall was named one of the _____ _____

    of the world.

Japan and China (cont.)

ACTIVITY 21 Drawing Conclusions

Name:_____

Date:_____

Teizo pulled on the main cord to maneuver his "Sky Dragon" into a better position. The cutting string was covered with small, sharp pieces of glass. It hadn't been easy gluing them to the string, but it had been worth it.

There was only one opponent left, holding tight to the strings of a large, rectangular construction with a grinning demon face painted on it. For fangs, the demon had two small knife blades sticking out if its muzzle. Teizo had watched those blades slice the strings of others, sending days of work crashing into a jumble of bamboo and paper onto the rocky ground.

Teizo gave a quick, skillful tug. Sky Dragon glided in front of the demon face, barely missing the fangs. The cutting string sawed against the demon's strings. With a loud snap, his opponent was left holding a tangle of limp cord as his demon sailed out of view. Teizo was the champion!

What traditional Japanese game was Teizo playing?

_____ a. Dragons and Demons

_____ b. Kite Fighting

_____ c. Sumo Wrestling

ACTIVITY 22 Fact and Opinion

Name:_____

Date:_____

A fact can be proved. An opinion is what you believe or think. Read the sentences below. Put "F" by the facts and "O" by the opinions.

_____ 1. Kites were invented in China 3,000 years ago.

_____ 2. The first kites were made by a general to use as weapons.

_____ 3. I think it's much better to use kites for fun than for war.

_____ 4. Kites loaded with explosives were used to frighten enemy soldiers.

_____ 5. Buddhist monks brought kites to Japan.

_____ 6. My favorite kites are the ones shaped like butterflies.

_____ 7. In Japan, they used to make some kites so big that it took 100 men to hold them.

Japan and China (cont.)

ACTIVITY 23 **Following Directions**

Name:_____

Date:_____

Haiku is a type of Japanese poetry. It is made up of 17 syllables arranged in three lines of 5, 7, and 5 syllables. The poems have a simple nature theme and have words that relate to the season.

Here is an example:

Lazy, heat-filled day,
Even sunflowers drooping,
Welcome, summertime!

Following the directions given above, write your own haiku poem.

_____

_____

_____

ACTIVITY 24 **Inference**

Name:_____

Date:_____

Read the paragraph, and then finish the story. Use your own paper if you need more room.

A famous Chinese folktale explains how the four great rivers of China came into being. Once upon a time, there was a great drought. All the crops were dying, and the people were starving. They prayed for help, but the Jade Emperor, the head of all the gods, ignored them. Four dragons—the Long Dragon, the Yellow Dragon, the Black Dragon, and the Pearl Dragon—defied the Jade Emperor and helped the people by scooping up water from the sea with their mouths and spraying it into the sky so that it became rain. The Jade Emperor was furious and wanted to punish them, so he told the Mountain God to put a mountain on top of each of the dragons. But the dragons got the better of the Jade Emperor by ...

_____

_____

_____

_____

_____

Japan and China (cont.)

ACTIVITY 25 Main Idea

Name:_____

Date:_____

Read the following paragraph. Then put a plus (+) next to the main idea.

China has one of the world's oldest uninterrupted civilizations. Forty-five-hundred-year-old turtle shells have been found with markings on them that look like Chinese writing. Archaeologists believe that Chinese civilization started with city-states in the Yellow River valley. Around 200 B.C., China became a unified empire. From then until the Communist Revolution in the mid-twentieth century, there was an unbroken line of emperors on the throne of China.

_____ 1. China has a very long history.

_____ 2. Some early Chinese wrote on turtle shells.

_____ 3. China began in the Yellow River valley.

ACTIVITY 26 Predicting Outcomes

Name:_____

Date:_____

Read the story, and then predict how the story ended. Write your prediction on the lines below. Use your own paper if you need more room.

There is a Japanese fairy tale that is very similar to the story of Snow White. It is the story of Princess Hase, who was good and beautiful and much loved. Her mother died, and her father remarried. Though she pretended to love the princess, Hase's stepmother was really jealous of her. The stepmother decided to kill Princess Hase by giving her a cup of poisoned fruit juice. However, the cups got mixed up, and Princess Hase's little half-brother drank the poison. After this, the stepmother hated Hase even more and blamed the princess for the death of her son. Finally, when Hase's father was away, the stepmother told a servant to take Hase out into the forest and kill her. The servant, however, built a house deep in the forest where he and his wife took care of the little girl. When the father came home, his wife said Princess Hase had done something terrible and run away. The father grieved for a long time. One day, to forget his sorrow for a while, he took a hunting party deep into the forest.

_____

_____

_____

Japan and China (cont.)

ACTIVITY 27 Sequencing

Name:_____

Date:_____

Ikebana is the Japanese art of flower arranging. *Heika* are arrangments in tall, thin vases. *Moribana* uses low, shallow containers. Every arrangement has three main elements: primary, secondary, and ornamental stems. In *moribana*, the primary stem is vertical; the secondary stem is slanted a bit and is near the primary stem. The ornamental stem is slanted even more and is placed to the front and right of the primary stem. Seen from above, the three stems form a right triangle with the secondary stem at the point of the right angle. Flowers are placed inside this triangle to fill out the shape.

Label the parts of the moribana arrangement diagrammed below and number them in sequence.

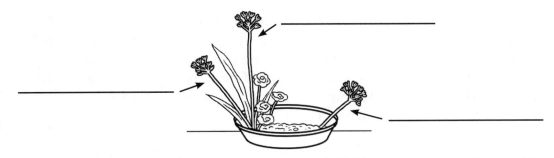

ACTIVITY 28 Summarizing

Name:_____

Date:_____

Read the following paragraph, and then write a summarizing sentence.

Getting an education in China is considered a privilege. Only since 1978 have all children in China been expected to go to school for at least nine years. Anyone who wishes to continue after that must pass several tests. Those who do not wish to take the tests, or who do not pass them, are expected to start working. To stay in school, students first take the entrance examination for senior middle schools or middle-level technical schools. Then after two, three, or four years, those who make it through these schools take the national college entrance examinations in July. Because of the difficulty of these tests, the month of July in China has been nicknamed "Black July."

Write a summarizing sentence. _____

_____

_____

_____

_____

Poetry and Plays

ACTIVITY 29 **Author's Purpose**

Name:_____

Date:_____

Read the following paragraphs. Decide if the author's purpose is to entertain, inform, or persuade. Then put a plus (+) next to the answer.

1. William Shakespeare lived in England during the reign of Queen Elizabeth I. He wrote numerous plays of all sorts, including tragedies, comedies, and historical dramas. In addition to being a writer, Shakespeare was also an actor. What he is remembered for, however, are his plays, which are still being performed nearly four hundred years after his death.

   _____ entertain   _____ inform   _____ persuade

2. Hilary swallowed nervously. In another moment, it would be time for her to go on. She twitched her costume into place and took a deep breath, hoping she wouldn't be sick. Oh, why had she let Megan talk her into being in this stupid play. She was going to be Juliet, no less. If she'd known Skyler was going to play Romeo, she'd never have tried out. It wasn't that she didn't like Skyler. He was a nice guy, but he just wasn't her idea of Romeo.

   _____ entertain   _____ inform   _____ persuade

ACTIVITY 30 **Compare and Contrast**

Name:_____

Date:_____

William Blake, a famous British poet who lived from 1757 to 1827, wrote two different poems entitled "Nurse's Song," one in a collection called *Songs of Innocence* and one in a collection called *Songs of Experience*. Read these excerpts from each, and then answer the questions below.

"Nurse's Song" from *Songs of Innocence*

When the voices of children are heard on the green
And laughing is heard on the hill,
My heart is at rest within my breast
And everything else is still.

Then come home my children: the sun is gone down
And the dews of night arise.
Come, come leave off play and let us away,
Till the morning appears in the sky.

"Nurse's Song from *Songs of Experience*

When the voices of children are heard on the green,
And whisperings are in the dale,
The days of my youth rise fresh in my mind,
My face turns green and pale.

Then come home, my children, the sun is gone down,
And the dews of night arise;
Your spring and your day are wasted in play,
And your winter and night in disguise.

1. Aside from the title, how are these two poems similar? _____

_____

2. How are they different? _____

3. Which one do you prefer?_____ Why? _____

_____

18

Poetry and Plays (cont.)

ACTIVITY 31 Context Clues

Name:_____

Date:_____

Choose a word from the Word Bank to replace the word in boldface in the following excerpt of a poem entitled "The Cricket" by Walt Whitman, a nineteenth-century American poet.

WORD BANK					
hushed	grasshopper	singer	whisper	bushes	softly singing

The humming bee purrs softly o'er his flowers;
    From lawn and **thicket** _____
The dogday **locust** singeth in the sun _____
    From hour to hour:
Each has his **bard**, and thou, ere day be done, _____
    Shall have no wrong.
So bright that **murmur** mid the insect crowd, _____
Muffled and lost in bottom grass, or loud _____
    By pale and picket:
Shall I not take to help me in my song
    A little **cooing** cricket? _____

ACTIVITY 32 Cause and Effect

Name:_____

Date:_____

Read the following, and then fill in the blanks below.

In Shakespeare's play, *A Midsummer Night's Dream*, Demetrius asks Hermia's father for her hand in marriage. However, Hermia loves Lysander, so the two of them decide to run away. Helena is in love with Demetrius. Demetrius goes after Hermia and Lysander. Helena follows Demetrius. In the forest, Oberon, the fairy king, hears Helena and Demetrius arguing. He decides to help. He sends Puck to find some magic flower juice that makes a sleeper fall in love with the first person he or she sees on waking. All four lovers are asleep in the forest. Puck puts the juice in Lysander's eyes by mistake. The first person he sees when he wakes is Helena. So now, Lysander is in love with Helena, who is in love with Demetrius, who is in love with Hermia, who is in love with Lysander. Oberon is angry with Puck for the mistake. Puck puts everyone to sleep again. He makes sure the boys are sleeping near the right girls this time and puts love juice in both Lysander and Demetrius's eyes. When they wake up, everyone is in love with the right person.

1. The juice from the magic flower causes sleepers to _____
_____.
2. The effect Oberon wanted was _____.
3. Instead, Puck put the juice in _____ eyes, which caused him to fall in love with _____.
4. When he realized his mistake, Puck causes everyone to _____.
5. He puts more drops in _____ and _____ eyes.
6. This causes everyone to be in love with _____.

Poetry and Plays (cont.)

ACTIVITY 33 **Character Analysis**

Name:_____

Date:_____

Read the following stanza from "The Cremation of Sam McGee," a ballad by Robert Service, who wrote many poems and stories about the Alaskan gold fields.

> Now Sam McGee was from Tennessee,
> Where the cotton blooms and blows.
> Why he left his home in the South to roam
> 'Round the Pole, God only knows.
> He was always cold, but the land of gold
> Seemed to hold him like a spell;
> Though he'd often say in his homely way
> That he'd "sooner live in hell."

1. Do you think Sam McGee was an educated man? _____ Why? _____

2. Who do you think Sam McGee was?

    _____ a. a farmer   _____ b. a tour guide   _____ c. a prospector

3. Is Sam McGee someone you'd like to meet? _____ Why or why not?_____

_____

ACTIVITY 34 **Details**

Name:_____

Date:_____

Read the following paragraph, and then answer the questions.

In the play *Pygmalion*, by George Bernard Shaw, the main character, Eliza Dolittle, is a flower seller in London. Professor Henry Higgins makes a bet with his friend, Colonel Pickering, saying he can teach Eliza the proper way to speak and pass her off as a lady. Eliza sees this as a chance to get a better job, maybe even in a flower shop. She works very hard and succeeds beyond Higgins' wildest dreams. However, he takes all the credit for her success. This makes Eliza angry, and she leaves. In the musical based on the play, Eliza eventually makes up with Higgins. In Shaw's play, she marries a young man named Freddy who is much nicer to her than Higgins ever was.

1. What is the name of Professor Higgins' friend?_____

2. With whom did Eliza end up in the original play? _____

3. With whom did she end up in the musical based on the play? _____

_____

4. What did Higgins teach Eliza? _____

5. What was Eliza's dream? _____

Poetry and Plays (cont.)

ACTIVITY 35 Drawing Conclusions

Name:_____

Date:_____

Read the following stanza of a poem by the American poet, Emily Dickinson, and then answer the questions below.

> Safe in their Alabaster Chambers—
> Untouched by Morning
> And untouched by Noon—
> Sleep the meek members of the Resurrection—
> Rafter of satin,
> And Roof of stone.

1. Who are the "meek members of the Resurrection" that Dickinson is talking about?

   _____

2. To what do the lines "Rafter of satin,/And Roof of stone" refer?

   _____

3. Why would the people she is writing about be "untouched" by morning or noon?

   _____

(*Hint:* Resurrection refers to the belief that, at the end of time, everyone who has died will be resurrected, or brought to life again. Alabaster is a kind of white stone that is often used to build monuments and tombs.)

ACTIVITY 36 Fact and Opinion

Name:_____

Date:_____

A fact can be proved. An opinion is what you believe or think. Read the sentences below. Put "F" by the facts and "O" by the opinions.

_____ 1. I think *The Importance of Being Earnest* by Oscar Wilde is a great play.

_____ 2. There are two men in the play who pretend to be Earnest.

_____ 3. Actually, there is no real Earnest in the play.

_____ 4. I think it is hilarious that the nurse confused a baby and a manuscript.

_____ 5. I agree with people who say Oscar Wilde was a very funny writer.

_____ 6. I've seen three different productions of *The Importance of Being Earnest*.

Poetry and Plays (cont.)

ACTIVITY 37 Following Directions

Name:_____

Date:_____

Read the following Robert Louis Stevenson poem "The Wind." It has six lines of four beats each (da-Dum, da-Dum, da-Dum, da-Dum),and an AABBCC rhyme pattern with the last two lines repeating, like a song chorus. Choose a nature theme such as "The Snow," "The Rain," or "The Night Sky," etc. On your own paper, write at least one verse about your subject using the same poetic form as Stevenson.

I saw you toss the kites on high
And blow the birds about the sky,
And all around I hear you pass,
Like ladies' skirts across the grass—
O wind, a-blowing all day long,
O wind, that sings so loud a song!

I saw the different things you did,
But always you yourself you hid.
I felt you push, I heard you call,
I could not see yourself at all—
O wind, a-blowing all day long,
O wind, that sings so loud a song!

O you that are so strong and cold,
O blower are you young or old?
Are you a beast of field and tree,
Or just a stronger child than me?
O wind, a-blowing all day long,
O wind, that sings so loud a song!

ACTIVITY 38 Inference

Name:_____

Date:_____

Read the following paragraph, and then answer the questions below.

The Inspector General is a very funny play by nineteenth-century Russian author, Nikolai Gogol. In it, the Mayor and a group of crooked officials in a small town are alarmed when they hear rumors that the "Inspector General" is coming to their town in disguise to look into their doings. They mistakenly think that a lowly clerk from Saint Petersburg, who arrived in town a few days earlier, is the Inspector in disguise. The Mayor and his cronies all have things to hide, so they wine and dine the clerk and give him all kinds of presents and bribes. The silly clerk does not realize that he is being mistaken for someone else. His servant figures out what is going on, and the two of them quickly leave town. In the last scene, two things occur, the first of which makes the Mayor and his friends angry and the second of which makes them afraid.

What do you think these two things are?

1. _____

_____

2. _____

_____

Poetry and Plays (cont.)

ACTIVITY 39 **Main Idea**

Name: _____

Date: _____

Read the paragraph below, and then put a plus (+) next to the main idea.

"All the world's a stage" is a very well-known saying. All over the world and throughout history, people have done all sorts of "play-acting." The first actors were cavemen who acted out their latest hunt around the campfire. In Ancient Greece, plays were considered sacred. Watching a tragedy, such as *Oedipus Rex*, was thought to be a cathartic experience that helped people get rid of their bad feelings. In medieval times, roving bands of players put on "morality plays," dramatizing the stories of the Bible for people who didn't know how to read. Dressing up and playing make-believe is a universal part of the human experience.

_____ a.   Even cavemen liked to act.

_____ b.   Watching a Greek play was a cathartic experience.

_____ c.   Plays and make-believe are things all people enjoy.

ACTIVITY 40 **Predicting Outcomes**

Name: _____

Date: _____

Read the following story, and then predict how you think the story ends.

In the one-act play called *The Ugly Duckling* by A.A. Milne, a king and queen are worried because their daughter, Princess Camilla, is very plain, or rather appears to be plain because of a spell put on her at birth. The spell says that only the eyes of true love will reveal her beauty. Her parents come up with a plan to marry her to a prince from a far-away land who doesn't know what she looks like. They force Camilla to trade places with her beautiful but silly maid, Dulcibella, before the prince arrives. When Prince Simon comes in, he is a very handsome, but silly, young man. He and Dulcibella hit it off right away. Princess Camilla bumps into Simon's servant, who is very nice but not as good-looking as the prince. Camilla tells him she has a secret, and he replies that he has a secret, too.

The play ends happily for all concerned. Predict how you think this happens.

_____

_____

_____

Bonus Activity: Read the play and see if your prediction was correct.

Poetry and Plays (cont.)

ACTIVITY 41 **Sequencing**

Name: _____

Date: _____

Robert Frost's poem, *Stopping by Woods on a Snowy Evening*, has a complicated rhyme scheme. It goes AABA, BBCB, CCDC, DDDD. The following stanzas are scrambled. Use the rhyme scheme to help you number them in sequence from 1 to 4.

a. _____ He gives his harness bell a shake
        To ask if there is some mistake.
        The only other sound's the sweep
        Of easy wind and downy flake.

d. _____ My little horse must think it queer
        To stop without a farmhouse near
        Between the woods and frozen lake
        The darkest evening of the year.

b. _____ Whose woods these are I think I know
        His house is in the village though;
        He will not see me stopping here
        To watch his woods fill up with snow.

c. _____ The woods are lovely, dark and deep.
        But I have promises to keep,
        And miles to go before I sleep,
        And miles to go before I sleep.

ACTIVITY 42 **Summarizing**

Name: _____

Date: _____

Read the following paragraph, and then write a summarizing sentence.

   Some people say that poetry is writing that sings. Prose is writing that talks. It tells a story or gives information, and it touches our hearts in a different way from poetry. There are many kinds of poems. There are rhyming poems, blank verses, haiku poems, and sonnets. There are limericks and nursery rhymes. There are long heroic epics and short, two-line couplets. Some poetry tells a story, and some prose stories have poetic language in them, but you can always tell the difference between the two.

Write a summarizing sentence. _____

_____

_____

_____

_____

Weather

ACTIVITY 43 **Author's Purpose**

Name:_____

Date:_____

Read the following paragraphs. Decide if the author's purpose is to entertain, inform, or persuade. Then put a plus (+) next to the answer.

1. Whether the weather is cold
   Or whether the weather is hot
   There's going to be weather
   Whatever the weather
   Whether we like it or not.

   _____ entertain

   _____ inform

   _____ persuade

2. Our trench coats stand up to the test
   Of the weather with which we are blessed
   A coat for all seasons
   From frying to freezin'
   Bob's trench coats are simply the best!

   _____ entertain

   _____ inform

   _____ persuade

ACTIVITY 44 **Compare and Contrast**

Name:_____

Date:_____

Read the following, and then fill in the Venn diagram below.

    Cumulus and nimbostratus are types of clouds. **Nimbostratus** are dark, low-level clouds that form a thick layer in the sky. These are the clouds that bring long, soaking rain in the summer and deep snow in the winter, the kind that lasts for days. **Cumulus** clouds look like floating cotton and have a lifetime of 5–40 minutes. Like nimbostratus clouds, they are formed of condensed water droplets and occur at about the same altitude. Cumulus clouds can build up into huge thunderheads and lead to spectacular summer storms.

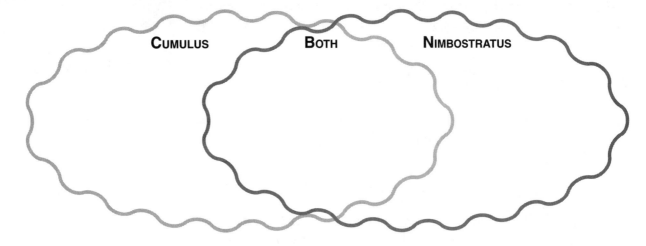

CUMULUS   BOTH   NIMBOSTRATUS

Weather (cont.)

ACTIVITY 45 **Context Clues**

Name:_____

Date:_____

Use context clues in the sentences to find the meaning of the words in bold. Put a plus (+) next to the answer.

1. *El Niño* refers to a weak, warm current appearing **annually** around Christmas time along the coast of Ecuador and Peru.

    _____ a. yearly   _____ b. occasionally   _____ c. unexpectedly

2. Every three to seven years, an *El Niño* event may last for many months, having important **consequences** worldwide.

    _____ a. likenesses   _____ b. effects   _____ c. attention

3. In the past forty years, there have been ten **significant** *El Niño* events recorded.

    _____ a. noteworthy   _____ b. boring   _____ c. usual

4. The worst, and most recent, *El Niño* event **transpired** in 1997 to 1998.

    _____ a. waited   _____ b. completed   _____ c. happened

5. Scientists **surmise** that the increase in *El Niño* severity is due to global warming.

    _____ a. hope   _____ b. fear   _____ c. guess

ACTIVITY 46 **Cause and Effect**

Name:_____

Date:_____

Read the following paragraph. Then, for each pair of sentences below, write a "C" if the sentence is a cause; write "E" if the sentence is an effect.

Hurricanes begin when the weather conditions are just right for a cluster of thunderstorms to form over a tropical ocean. If such a cluster remains long enough, it organizes into a tropical depression, with winds of up to 42 miles per hour. If a tropical depression increases to winds of 43 to 74 miles per hour, it is a tropical storm. A tropical storm is given a name and watched closely, by satellite, to see if it gets worse and begins to have the telltale circular shape of a hurricane. If the air pressure continues to drop, the wind rises to above 75 miles per hour, and a true hurricane is born.

_____ 1. Winds rise to 75+ miles per hour.
_____ 2. The pressure continues to drop.

_____ 3. A cluster of thunderstorms forms over a tropical ocean.
_____ 4. The weather conditions are just right.

_____ 5. The telltale circular shape begins forming.
_____ 6. A tropical storm gets worse.

_____ 7. A cluster begins to organize into a tropical depression.
_____ 8. Winds increase to 23 to 42 miles an hour.

26

Weather(cont.)

 **ACTIVITY 47** **Character Analysis**

Name:_____

Date:_____

Read the following poem that uses both *metaphor* and *personification*. Then answer the questions below.

April and May by Anne Robinson

April is a laundress
Mixing silver suds
To rinse the lacy dance frocks
Of apple-blossom buds.

May Day is the nursemaid
Who looks the flowers over
And ties their little bonnets
On the buttercup and clover.

1. To which person does the poet compare April? _____

2. What character traits does the poet seem to ascribe to May? _____

_____

3. Think of another month of the year and the kind of weather it has.

Month: _____ What kind of a person would you use as a metaphor

for that month? _____

ACTIVITY 48 **Details**

Name:_____

Date:_____

Look at the list of weather conditions listed below, and the symbol for each. Study the weather map and a map of the United States that shows state boundaries, and then answer the questions below.

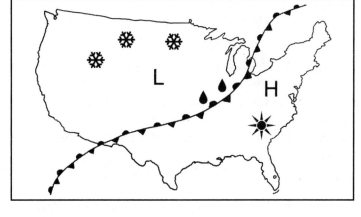

Map Key

H - High Pressure   L - Low Pressure

⌁ - Weather Front   ❋ - Snow

💧 - Rain   ☀ - Sun

1. Over what states is there a low-pressure zone? _____

2. Over what states is there a high-pressure zone? _____

3. Is it snowing anywhere? _____ Where?_____

4. Is it raining anywhere? _____ Where?_____

5. Through what states is there a weather front?_____

Weather (cont.)

ACTIVITY 49 Drawing Conclusions

Name: _____

Date: _____

Read the following paragraph. Then read each question and put a plus (+) next to the answer.

Rainbows are one of the loveliest weather effects. Morning rainbows always show up in the west. Evening rainbows always show up in the east. Sometimes, you can see short rainbows, called sun dogs, around the sun if there is a lot of humidity in the air. For a rainbow to appear, the sun cannot be more than halfway up the sky. Sometimes, you can see a double, or even triple, rainbow if the angle of the sun and amount of rain are just right.

1. You see a rainbow in the west,
   so you know it is:
   _____ a. morning.
   _____ b. afternoon.
   _____ c. evening.

2. The angle of the sun is just right.
   It is raining. You see:
   _____ a. a sun dog.
   _____ b. a mirage.
   _____ c. a double rainbow.

3. In the evening, you look for a rainbow:
   _____ a. in the east.
   _____ b. in the west.
   _____ c. straight up.

4. The sun is at high noon, and it is
   raining. You see a rainbow:
   _____ a. in the east.
   _____ b. in the west.
   _____ c. nowhere.

ACTIVITY 50 Fact and Opinion

Name: _____

Date: _____

A fact can be proved. An opinion is what you believe or think. Read the sentences below. Put "F" by the facts and "O" by the opinions.

_____ 1. Where Earth's weather occurs is called the atmosphere.

_____ 2. Weather conditions control many aspects of our lives.

_____ 3. I think it would be boring to live where the weather was always the same.

_____ 4. The amount of precipitation a place has determines what grows there.

_____ 5. Wouldn't it be wonderful if we could find a way to control the weather?

_____ 6. The prevailing weather in a place is called its climate.

_____ 7. Huge climatic changes may have been what killed

the dinosaurs.

Weather (cont.)

ACTIVITY 51 **Following Directions**   Name: _____

Date: _____

Follow the directions below to construct a tornado maker.

1. Get two large, clear plastic soda bottles.

2. Fill one bottle with water and a few drops of food coloring.

3. Turn the second bottle upside down over the first one.

4. Use packing or duct tape to tape the two bottle necks together.

5. Turn the tornado maker upside down and swirl it around.

6. The water will flow from the top bottle to the bottom with a spiral motion that looks just like a tornado.

Bonus Project: Have races to see whose tornado bottle empties the fastest.

- -

ACTIVITY 52 **Inference**   Name: _____

Date: _____

Read the story, and then answer the questions below.

"I don't like the look of that sky," Grandpa Earl said to Rosie. He began walking faster, his eyes glued to the dark clouds overhead. "No, sir, I don't like it at all. It's got that greenish look that always comes with bad news right behind it."

"What kind of bad news?" Asked Rosie.

"The worst kind. You go find your ma and tell her to get you and your brother down to the cellar. I'm going to get old Bessie. The barn would never stand up to a real blow. Go on, now. Scat!"

Rosie ran as fast as she could, her eyes on the sky. Every once in a while, a long, black snake of cloud wound down from the bottom of the roiling mass, then got sucked back up. Every time it happened, the snake got a little longer. Grandpa was right. Bad news was coming, all right, and coming fast.

1. Where do you think this story is taking place? _____ Why do you think this?

   _____

2. What kind of "bad news" does Grandpa mean? _____

3. What do you think is going to happen next? _____

   _____

Weather (cont.)

ACTIVITY 53   Main Idea

Name:_____

Date:_____

Read the paragraph below, and then put a plus (+) next to the main idea.

If you want to know what the weather is going to be, look up, down, and all around you. People have been reading weather signs for thousands of years. Farmers learn to tell when spring is just around the corner by the feel of the air and the smell of new growth. Sailors at sea can spot a hurricane brewing by studying the currents in the ocean and the clouds in the sky. Many native peoples know when a hard winter is coming by watching the behavior of animals and the growth pattern of certain plants. Meteorology, with all its gauges, graphs, and instruments, is a fairly new science, but predicting the weather is an art as old as the hills.

_____ 1. People have been predicting the weather for a long time in many ways.

_____ 2. Sailors always know when a hurricane is coming.

_____ 3. Some animals and plants can give clues to future weather.

ACTIVITY 54   Predicting Outcomes

Name:_____

Date:_____

Climate has to do with many factors. One is latitude. Places closer to the equator generally have a warmer climate. Places closer to the Poles generally have a colder climate. Climate also has to do with altitude. Places at high altitudes have a colder climate than those closer to sea level. Also, areas on the side of a mountain range that is nearest the sea tend to be wetter; areas on the side of the mountains away from the sea are usually very dry.

After reading the paragraph above, read the following descriptions of the location of each place. Predict what the weather is like in each, and put a plus (+) next to the most likely answer.

1. This area is about halfway between the equator and the North Pole. It is between the mountains and the Pacific Ocean. Most of it is at sea level.

_____ a. wet and warm   _____ b. dry and hot   _____ c. wet and cold

2. This area is below sea level and on the far side of a mountain range from the ocean. It is closer to the equator than the North Pole.

_____ a. dry and cold   _____ b. wet and hot   _____ c. dry and hot

3. This area is nearer the North Pole than the equator. It is on the ocean side of the mountains and at a very high altitude.

_____ a. wet and cold   _____ b. dry and cold   _____ c. wet and warm

Weather (cont.)

ACTIVITY 55 Sequencing

Name:_____

Date:_____

Hail is formed in summer thunderstorm clouds. Droplets of supercooled (really cool but not frozen) water cling to particles of dust in the top part of a thunderhead. As these pre-hailstones form, they become heavy and start to fall. As they fall, they evaporate a little while going through the warmer midsection of the cloud. They get caught by an updraft and are then lifted back into the upper section of the cloud. The hailstones once again gather more droplets and grow even bigger. They start to fall again and, until they reach a certain size, are thrown up into the cloud over and over again. This cycle continues until the hailstones are heavy enough to overcome the updraft. At this point, the hail falls out of the cloud and onto the ground.

Number the steps below in sequence from 1 to 8.

_____ a. The pre-hailstones become too heavy for the top of the cloud.
_____ b. They gather more droplets and grow even bigger.
_____ c. Supercooled droplets begin clinging to dust particles in the top of a thundercloud.
_____ d. They get thrown up into the cloud over and over again.
_____ e. They become too heavy for the updraft.
_____ f. They start to fall and also to evaporate a little.
_____ g. They get caught by an updraft.
_____ h. They fall to the ground.

ACTIVITY 56 Summarizing

Name:_____

Date:_____

Read the following paragraph, and then write a summarizing sentence below.

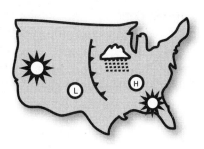

For a long time, people have wished they could control the weather. The next best thing, however, is to be able to predict it accurately. Thanks to satellites in the sky, complex equipment, and instant communication throughout the world, we are able to do so, at least part of the time. As bad as Hurricane Katrina was, it would have been much worse if there had been no warning of it. We control the weather in our houses, and we can watch weather happening from satellite cameras. Who knows what the future will bring?

Write a summarizing sentence. _____

_____

_____

_____

Nutrition

ACTIVITY 57   Author's Purpose

Name:_____

Date:_____

Read the following paragraphs. Decide if the author's purpose is to entertain, inform, or persuade. Then put a plus (+) next to the answer.

1. *Salmon Soufflé:* A delectable, melt-in-your-mouth appetizer made with freshly caught, wild Alaskan salmon, organic eggs, and cream from our restaurant cow, Bessie. Served in individual dishes with a delicately seasoned lemon sauce. This is a house specialty that you will find nowhere else in the world.

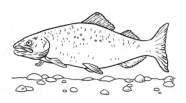

_____ entertain   _____ inform   _____ persuade

2. *Salmon Loaf*: Wild-caught Alaskan salmon. Organic ingredients. Baked fresh daily. Calories per serving: 750. Fat content: 4 grams. Fulfills daily requirements of Omega 6 fatty acids, vitamin A, and protein. Contains: wheat, dairy, and peanut oil.

_____ entertain   _____ inform   _____ persuade

ACTIVITY 58   Compare and Contrast

Name:_____

Date:_____

Read the following, and then fill in the Venn diagram below.

Donna wanted fajitas for dinner. Stella wanted a chicken burrito.

"Here," said Mother, getting out chicken, refried beans (frijoles), lettuce, tomatoes, cheese, salsa, green peppers, and onions. "You can each make what you want."

Donna fried strips of chicken, peppers, and onions while Stella warmed up the frijoles. Then, each girl took a tortilla and began piling on food.

"Chicken, peppers, onions, tomatoes, and salsa. Yum!" said Donna as she took a big bite.

Stella piled on some chicken strips, some refried beans, lettuce, tomatoes, cheese, and salsa on her tortilla. "I love do-it-yourself food!" she agreed with her sister.

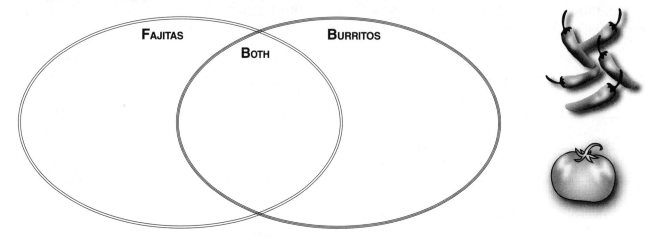

FAJITAS   BOTH   BURRITOS

32

Nutrition (cont.)

ACTIVITY 59 Context Clues

Name: _____

Date: _____

Use context clues to pick the right definition from the Word Bank for the bold words in the sentences below.

mystery	invented	poisonous
unusual	needs	

1. Vegetables are one of the **requirements** of a balanced diet.

   _____

2. Many countries have **developed** complex vegetable dishes.

   _____

3. Some vegetables, such as hearts-of-palm, are quite **exotic**.

   _____

4. Rhubarb is a plant that has only one part that is not **toxic**.

   _____

5. How someone figured out what was safe to eat is a **conundrum**.

   _____

ACTIVITY 60 Cause and Effect

Name: _____

Date: _____

Read the following paragraph, and then write the letter of each effect beside its cause.

There are many diseases caused by certain kinds of vitamin deficiencies. For instance, scurvy is caused by too little vitamin C and leads to gum disease and tooth loss. Rickets, a disease in which the bones become deformed, is caused by not getting enough vitamin D. Too little vitamin A can impair your eyesight. Too little vitamin B-6 can cause hair loss. Not enough magnesium causes your heartbeat to become irregular. Too little selenium can lead to an enlarged heart. If you don't get enough calcium, you're liable to have leg cramps. So you see, it's a good idea to eat a variety of nutritious foods.

1. Vitamin A deficiency causes _____.
2. Magnesium deficiency causes _____.
3. Vitamin C deficiency causes _____.
4. Calcium deficiency causes _____.
5. Vitamin B-6 deficiency causes _____.
6. Selenium deficiency causes _____.
7. Vitamin D deficiency causes _____.

a. irregular heartbeat
b. tooth loss
c. bone deformity
d. hair loss
e. bad eyesight
f. leg cramps
g. an enlarged heart

Nutrition (cont.)

ACTIVITY 61 Character Analysis

Name: _____

Date: _____

Read the following dialogue, and then fill in the blanks below.

"Here, let me show you how it's done!" Salizar grabbed the rolling pin out of Raul's hand.

"Hey, Mr. Gonzales put me in charge of rolling out the tortillas," Raul protested, grabbing the rolling pin back.

"Yes, but my father is a chef. I know the right way to do it," Salizar insisted, making another swipe at the rolling pin. Raul held it out of his reach, glaring. "Oh, come on, Raul. Please let me do it. I love making tortillas. Please?"

Raul thought a minute. "I like to make them, too, and it's my job, but I guess we could take turns."

"Great!" said Salizar. "I get to go first!"

1. Think of three character traits to describe Raul.

   _____ _____ _____

2. Think of three character traits to describe Salizar.

   _____ _____ _____

3. Are you more like Salizar or Raul? _____

ACTIVITY 62 Details

Name: _____

Date: _____

Read the paragraph, and then find the missing words in the word search puzzle.

Fruits and vegetables are both delicious and nutritious. The pigments that make beets and strawberries red, kiwis and kale green, peaches and pumpkins orange, and lemons and summer squash yellow are powerful antioxidants that help keep cancer cells from forming. Both fruits and vegetables are also high in vitamins and other nutrients needed for great health. Fruits and vegetables are complex carbohydrates, or "carbs," so they give you a lot of energy without a "sugar high." So next time snack time rolls around, pass on the candy bar and try an apple or carrot instead. Your body will thank you for it.

1. The _____ in fruits and vegetables fight cancer.
2. These pigments are called _____.
3. Both fruits and vegetables are high in _____.
4. and other _____.
5. _____ carbohydrates are the best kind.
6. The abbreviation for carbohydrates is _____.
7. Instead of candy, eat an _____.

S	N	I	M	A	T	I	V	K	M
B	Q	N	I	N	Z	A	L	W	I
F	P	Y	O	T	P	F	S	U	D
M	I	S	S	I	Z	T	Y	C	G
T	G	T	C	O	M	P	L	E	X
N	M	N	L	X	R	C	O	L	E
M	E	E	B	I	P	Q	U	C	T
P	N	I	W	D	Z	V	Y	J	E
Y	T	R	R	A	A	S	A	M	L
I	S	T	U	N	N	V	Z	A	P
H	I	U	N	T	A	S	Y	G	P
P	A	N	X	S	B	R	A	C	A

Nutrition (cont.)

ACTIVITY 63 **Drawing Conclusions**

Name: _____

Date: _____

Read the following paragraph, and then answer the questions below.

"Set them both down here," said Mom. "Wow, you picked a couple of big ones!"

"I get to carve the eyes on both of them, don't forget," said Natasha. "And Morgan does the mouths and noses."

"How do you make a pie out of one of these things?" asked Morgan as Mom cut a lid in the first one and then began scooping out the seeds.

"You cook it, mash the insides, stir in some eggs, milk, and spices, pour it into a crust, and bake it," Mom explained.

"Sounds like fun," said Morgan.

"Let's just carve one and make a pie out of the other," suggested Natasha.

1. What are the "big ones" in the first sentence? _____

2. Near what holiday is the story taking place? _____

3. What are Morgan and Natasha doing? _____

_____

ACTIVITY 64 **Fact and Opinion**

Name: _____

Date: _____

A fact can be proved. An opinion is what you believe or think. Read the sentences below. Put "F" by the facts and "O" by the opinions.

_____ 1. I think yogurt is a great snack food.

_____ 2. Some people who are allergic to other dairy products can eat yogurt.

_____ 3. This is because of the acidophilus bacteria that are in it.

_____ 4. The bacteria digest lactose, the part of milk to which many people are sensitive.

_____ 5. My favorite kind of yogurt is made from goat's milk.

_____ 6. For centuries, people all over the world have eaten yogurt.

_____ 7. It may very well be that eating yogurt helps you live longer.

Nutrition (cont.)

 **ACTIVITY 65** **Following Directions**

Name:_____

Date:_____

Here's a snack that tastes great and is good for you, too. Take a large sweet potato. Peel it and cut it into french-fry strips. Drizzle 2 tablespoons of olive oil over the top. Sprinkle with 1 teaspoon of dillweed and 1/2 teaspoon of salt. Spread on a cookie sheet. Bake at 450°F for 15 minutes. Then broil for 10 minutes, turning once after 5 minutes.

Fill in the gaps in the recipe below.

SWEET POTATO FRIES

Take one large sweet potato.
_____ it and cut it into french-fry _____.
Drizzle with:
2 _____ olive oil   _____ teaspoon dillweed
1/2 teaspoon _____
Spread on a _____ _____.
Bake at _____°F for _____ minutes.
Broil for _____ minutes, turning _____ after _____ minutes.
ENJOY!

ACTIVITY 66 **Inference**

Name:_____

Date:_____

Read the following, and then answer the questions below.

"Tonight's the big potluck supper," said Hailey. "Mom's going to be late getting home from work, so she wants us to make something for it."

"What?" asked George.

"I don't know. She said to look around and see what we can come up with."

George looked in the refrigerator. Hailey looked on the shelves.

"Here's a can of olives and some peaches," she said.

"Here's some leftover meatloaf and a couple of carrots and half a cucumber," George added. "And some chopped-up tomatoes from the tacos last night."

"Here's baking chocolate and olive oil and vinegar. Say, there's still some lettuce in the garden. I saw it when I was watering."

"Great. That makes it easy to figure out what to make," said George.

"It sure does. Let's get going. The potluck starts in a half hour," said Hailey.

1. What did George and Hailey decide to make? _____

2. What three ingredients are they not likely to use?

_____ _____ _____

Nutrition (cont.)

 **Main Idea**

Name:_____

Date:_____

Read the paragraph below, and then put a plus (+) next to the main idea.

One of the biggest secrets to losing weight is: Don't eat too little. This is because nature has programmed our bodies to protect us from starving in times of famine. So if someone cuts back too much on their food intake, this natural defense kicks in and slows his or her metabolism. People who do this often find that they gain, rather than lose, weight. It is better to eat lots of good, healthy food such as fruits, vegetables, and whole grains than to restrict calories. You'll feel much better, and you'll slim down, too.

_____ 1. Eating well is better for weight loss than eating too little.

_____ 2. Whole grains are good for dieting.

_____ 3. Bodies have strange safety mechanisms.

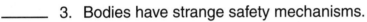

ACTIVITY 68 **Predicting Outcomes**

Name:_____

Date:_____

Latasha likes junk food; the junkier the better. Twinkies? Bring them on. Candy bars? She loves them. Oh, she eats a good meal now and then, but about 80% of her diet is cookies and chips and sodas and fast food. Tracy is just the opposite. She doesn't like sweet foods very much. She'll take a plate of spinach over a plate of Oreos any day. Her idea of a great snack is carrot sticks and yogurt dip. Sure, Tracy will have a donut or a bowl of ice cream now and then, but probably 80 percent of her diet is what Latasha refers to as "rabbit food."

1. Whom do you predict has better health, Latasha or Tracy? _____

2. Whom do you predict has more energy, Latasha or Tracy? _____

3. Whom do you predict has better grades, Latasha or Tracy? _____

4. Why?_____

5. What percentage of your diet is junk food? _____

6. How do you predict your health will be, based on your diet? _____

Nutrition (cont.)

ACTIVITY 69 **Sequencing**

Name: _____

Date: _____

As many as one-third of the people in the United States suffer from chronic **dehydration**, or lack of enough water in their body. The best way to avoid dehydration is to drink at least eight 8-ounce glasses of water every day. This sounds like a lot, but if you drink a 16-ounce glass of water ten minutes before and a 16-ounce glass of water ten minutes after each meal, as well as a glass at mid-morning and one when you get home from school, you'll get all eight in. Try it sometime and see how it feels.

Look at the activities at the left. List them on the schedule at the right. Expect meals to take half an hour. Check each item off as you enter it on the schedule.

___ Drink 1 glass of water	___ Brush teeth	7:00 a.m. Get up	3:30 School over
___ Brush teeth	___ Drink 1 glass of water	7:10 _____	4:00 Home
___ Drink 1 glass of water	___ Homework	7:20 _____	4:10 _____
___ Watch TV	___ Drink 1 glass of water	7:30 Breakfast	5:00 _____
___ Drink 1 glass of water	___ Afternoon break	8:10 _____	5:50 _____
___ Morning break	___ Drink 1 glass of water	8:30 School starts	6:00 Dinner
___ Drink 1 glass of water		10:00 _____	6:40 _____
___ Piano practice		10:15 _____	7:00 _____
___ Drink 1 glass water		11:50 _____	8:00 _____
		Noon Lunch	9:50 _____
		12:40 _____	10:00 Bedtime
		2:30 _____	

ACTIVITY 70 **Summarizing**

Name: _____

Date: _____

Read the following paragraph, and then write a summarizing sentence on the lines below.

There are three basic things necessary for life: air, water, and food. Without them, we cannot live. Most plants get their food from sunlight and nutrients in the soil. Animals, including humans, can't eat rocks or turn sunlight into food. We have to get food from other living things. Except for the chemicals that are added, everything we eat was once alive. Even heavily processed foods contain ingredients that once grew in a field or were some part of an animal. The next time you have a BLT sandwich, think about the pig that became the bacon, the plants that produced the lettuce and tomato, and the wheat that became the bread. Remember to say thank you to all the plants and animals who make it possible for you to eat and live.

Write a summarizing sentence. _____

_____

_____

_____

Greek and Roman Myths

ACTIVITY 71 Author's Purpose

Name:_____

Date:_____

Read the following posters. Decide if the author's purpose is to entertain, inform, or persuade. Then put a plus (+) next to the answer.

1.
A performance of the famous Greek tragedy, ***Oedipus Rex,*** will be held Friday, April 14, 8:00 P.M. at Centennial Hall.

TICKETS
$10 pre-purchase
$12 at the door
$6.00 for students

2.
Everyone loves their mother, but for ***Oedipus Rex,*** this was a tragic mistake. Find out why at the performance of this famous Greek play this Friday at Centennial Hall.

Call 555-5678 for tickets.

1. _____ a. entertain

_____ b. inform

_____ c. persuade

2. _____ a. entertain

_____ b. inform

_____ c. persuade

ACTIVITY 72 Compare and Contrast

Name:_____

Date:_____

Read the following, and then fill in the Venn diagram below.

Two well-known Greek gods are Ares and Hermes. Both were the sons of Zeus. Ares' mother was Hera. Hermes' mother was Maia, one of the daughters of the Titan, Atlas. Ares was the god of war and was shown wearing armor and armed with a spear. His special birds were barn owls, woodpeckers, and the vulture. Hermes was the god of messengers and travelers. He was usually portrayed wearing a winged cap and winged sandals and carrying a staff. Roosters and tortoises were his sacred animals.

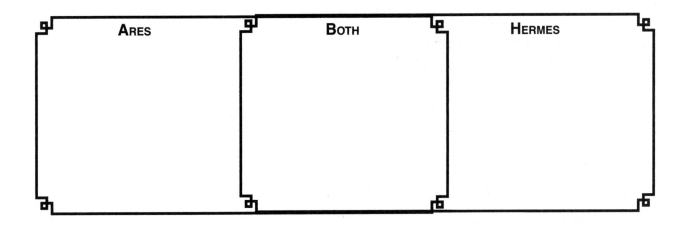

ARES   BOTH   HERMES

Greek and Roman Myths (cont.)

ACTIVITY 73 Context Clues

Name:_____

Date:_____

Choose a word or phrase from the Word Bank to replace the word in boldface in each sentence. Look for context clues to help you choose the right word.

WORD BANK					
thought to be	worshipped	thrived	gave	came out	dressed

1. Worship of the goddess Athena **flourished** in ancient Greece. _____

2. Athena was **revered** as the goddess of law and reason. _____

3. According to legend, Athena **emerged** fully grown from Zeus's forehead.

   _____

4. Athena was **considered** the patron of the city of Athens. _____

5. Athena is often shown **garbed** in a helmet and a goatskin breastplate.

   _____

6. According to legend, one of the gifts Athena **bestowed** on Athens was the olive tree.

   _____

ACTIVITY 74 Cause and Effect

Name:_____

Date:_____

Greek deities were believed to be the cause of many of the effects that are observed in nature. On the left is a description of some Greek gods and goddesses. On the right are some natural phenomena that they were thought to cause. Choose which god or goddess the Greeks would think caused each effect.

_____ 1. Zeus, who carries thunderbolts in a quiver on his back

_____ 2. Apollo, who drives the sun chariot

_____ 3. Demeter, who mourns for her daughter six months of the year

_____ 4. Iris, who carries messages from heaven to earth via a colorful bridge

_____ 5. Poseidon, who is in charge of all the oceans of the world

a. a tidal wave

b. rainbows

c. storms and lightning

d. sunrise and sunset

e. winter

Greek and Roman Myths (cont.)

ACTIVITY 75 Character Analysis

Name: _____

Date: _____

"Please, Father, let me drive the horses. I'm sure I can handle them."

"No, Phaethon, you're not strong enough," said Helius, god of the sun.

"But no one believes me when I say I'm your son," Phaethon argued. "Please? Just once?"

Helius sighed. "Very well. If you promise to be very careful and stay on the path. If you get too close to the earth, it will catch on fire; if you get too far away, it will freeze."

"I know, I know. Oh, thank you, Father!" Phaethon ran to his father's stable to hitch up the sun chariot. "Wait'll the guys see this," he gloated. "I'll dip down just a little bit—just enough so they can really see it's me. Father will never notice."

1. List three character traits for Phaethon.

   _____ _____ _____

2. What do you think happened to Phaethon? _____

   _____

ACTIVITY 76 Details

Name: _____

Date: _____

The planets of the solar system were named for Roman gods who were also Greek gods under another name. Using the details listed, match each planet with the corresponding Greek name.

_____ 1. Zeus, most powerful of all the gods

_____ 2. Ares, the god of war

_____ 3. Poseidon, the god of the seas

_____ 4. Hades, the god of the underworld

_____ 5. Gaia, the mother of all

_____ 6. Hermes, the messenger god, friend of Apollo

_____ 7. Aphrodite, the goddess of love

_____ 8. Ouranos, god of the sky

_____ 9. Kronos, father of Zeus

a. Mercury, closest to the sun

b. Venus, thought to help in romance

c. Earth, the only planet with life

d. Mars, the "red star of battle"

e. Jupiter, the biggest planet

f. Saturn, planet closest to Jupiter

g. Uranus, a gas giant

h. Neptune, appears blue

i. Pluto, the darkest planet

Greek and Roman Myths (cont.)

ACTIVITY 77 **Drawing Conclusions**

Name:_____

Date:_____

Read the following, and then answer the question below.

Ceres was the Roman goddess of grain and weather. Her daughter was Proserpina. One day, as Proserpina was picking flowers, the earth opened, and Pluto, god of the underworld, raced out in a chariot, snatched up Proserpina, and drove back with her to his kingdom. Ceres searched high and low for her daughter. While she was searching, rain no longer fell, and crops no longer grew. The people were starving. They prayed to Jupiter, asking him to reason with Ceres. Ceres refused to do anything until she found out what had become of her daughter. Jupiter discovered where Proserpina was, but he could not get her back because anyone who eats in the underworld has to stay there, and she had eaten some pomegranate seeds. Pluto took pity on Ceres and agreed that, each year, Proserpina only had to stay in the underworld a month for each of the six seeds she ate. For those six months, Ceres is happy, and the world rejoices. For the other six, while Proserpina is in the underworld, she is sad, and the world shares her woe.

Myths like this are made up to explain natural happenings. What do you think this story was

supposed to explain? _____

_____

ACTIVITY 78 **Fact and Opinion**

Name:_____

Date:_____

A fact can be proved. An opinion is what you believe or think. Read the sentences below. Put "F" by the facts and "O" by the opinions.

_____ 1. Greek and Roman myths have a lot of similarities.

_____ 2. Greek names are much prettier than Roman ones.

_____ 3. The Greeks did not revere their god of war as much as the

Romans did.

_____ 4. Both Greeks and Romans celebrated many religious and cultural events.

_____ 5. I'd like to have gone to a Roman school and had holidays all the time.

_____ 6. Many modern traditions have roots in Greek and Roman times.

_____ 7. Of all the Roman holidays, I think I would have liked Saturnalia best.

_____ 8. Saturnalia celebrated the winter solstice and was similar to Christmas.

Greek and Roman Myths (cont.)

ACTIVITY 79 **Following Directions**

Name: _____

Date: _____

1. Think of a natural event about which you are curious. _____

2. Think up a good name for a god or goddess. _____

3. What does this god or goddess do? _____

4. Think of a story explaining your natural event that involves your god or goddess. Use your own paper if you need more room. _____

_____

_____

_____

_____

Bonus Activity : Put together a book of "class myths."

ACTIVITY 80 **Inference**

Name: _____

Date: _____

Read the following Greek tale, and then answer the questions below.

Arion was a gifted flute player from Corinth. He won all the prizes at a music festival in Sicily. On his way home from the festival, he ran into a big problem. The sailors on his ship decided they wanted his prize money. They told him he could either jump overboard, or they would throw him into the sea. Arion didn't care for either choice, but he knew he couldn't change the sailors' minds. He asked to be allowed to play his flute one last time, after which he would jump. He played very beautifully. When he jumped, there were some friendly creatures in the water that had been attracted by his flute playing. They rescued Arion and took him to Corinth much faster than the ship was sailing. Arion enjoyed his ride very much, though it was hard to stay on such slippery beasts.

1. Whom do you think Arion's rescuers were? _____

2. What do you think happened when the ship got to Corinth, and the sailors went to report Arion's "tragic accident" to the king? _____

Greek and Roman Myths (cont.)

ACTIVITY 81 **Main Idea**

Name:_____

Date:_____

Read the paragraph below, and then put a plus (+) next to the main idea.

Many modern words and sayings come from Greek and Roman myths. The verb "tantalize," for example, comes from the story of King Tantalus who angered one of the gods and was punished by being given a terrible hunger and thirst. He was put in a place where he could see water and fruit but could not reach them. "Proud as a peacock" relates to the peacock being the bird of Hera, the haughty queen of the Greek gods. "Mercurial," means changeable, which comes from Mercury, a very changeable god. "Hygiene" comes from Hygeia, the goddess of health.

_____ 1. Hygeia and Mercury are Greek and Roman deities.

_____ 2. Being "proud as a peacock" means very haughty.

_____ 3. Many words and sayings have come to us from ancient Greece and Rome.

ACTIVITY 82 **Predicting Outcomes**

Name:_____

Date:_____

Pelias, a wicked king, was worried about his future. So he consulted the Oracle at Delphi, who warned him to beware of any man he saw wearing only one sandal. Years later, the hero, Jason, came to Pelias' palace. Just before he got there, Jason helped an old woman cross a river and lost one of his sandals in the water. The woman was really the goddess Hera. She warned him about Pelias and told him what to do. When Jason came to Pelias' kingdom, Pelias saw that Jason had only one sandal and remembered the prophecy. Pelias pretended to welcome Jason. While they were talking, Pelias asked Jason what he would do if he met the man whom he knew would be his downfall. Just as Hera had told him to do, Jason answered that he would send that man after the Golden Fleece, because it was a quest from which no one had ever returned.

1. What do you think Pelias did? _____

_____

2. How do you think the story turned out? _____

_____

_____

Greek and Roman Myths (cont.)

ACTIVITY 83 Sequencing

Name:_____

Date:_____

Heracles (HAIR-uh-klees) was a Greek hero. (He was known in Rome as Hercules.) To make up for a terrible crime he had committed, Heracles performed twelve labors for a king named Eurystheus. In order, Heracles killed a lion and a many-headed snake called a hydra; captured a hind, a female red deer; caught a wild boar; cleaned out a really dirty stable; chased off some nasty birds; captured a bull and some man-eating horses; acquired the belt of an Amazon queen; kidnapped some cows; found some special apples; and captured Cerberus, the three-headed dog that guards the gate to the underworld.

Match each letter of the name of the Labors of Heracles on the right to its proper number on the left. Use a reference source if you need help.

_____ Labor 1   _____ Labor 7   a. The Erymanthean Boar   g. The Lernaean Hydra

_____ Labor 2   _____ Labor 8   b. The Stymphalian Birds   h. The Cretan Bull

_____ Labor 3   _____ Labor 9   c. The Augean Stables   i. The Apples of the Hesperides

_____ Labor 4   _____ Labor 10   d. The Nemean Lion   j. The Hind of Ceryneia

_____ Labor 5   _____ Labor 11   e. The Belt of Hippolyta   k. The Wild Mares of Diomedes

_____ Labor 6   _____ Labor 12   f. Cerberus   l. Geryon's Cattle

ACTIVITY 84 Summarizing

Name:_____

Date:_____

Read the following paragraph, and then write a summarizing sentence below.

One of the reasons we know so many Greek legends is because of a poet named Homer and an unknown scribe. Homer lived in Greece in the eighth century B.C. He composed the *Iliad*, the story of the Trojan War, and the *Odyssey*, the story of the Greek hero Odysseus's journey home after the Trojan War ended. These epic poems tell us a great deal about the way the ancient Greeks acted and what they believed. Homer was blind, so he could only tell the stories to his audience. It was left to someone else to write them down. No one knows who the person was who first transcribed these poems onto paper nearly three thousand years ago. We do know that if he or she hadn't bothered to do so, we wouldn't be able to study and enjoy them today.

Write a summarizing sentence. _____

_____

_____

_____

Outer Space

ACTIVITY 85 **Author's Purpose**

Name:_____

Date:_____

Read the following paragraphs. Decide if the author's purpose is to entertain, inform, or persuade. Then put a plus (+) next to the answer.

1. Black holes are thought to be stars that have such strong gravitational fields that even light cannot escape from them. Because no light comes from them, black holes can't actually be seen, but we're pretty sure they're there. Astronomers have located several systems that act like they have binary stars—two stars that orbit each other—yet there is only one star visible. They think the other, invisible, star is a black hole.

    _____ entertain   _____ inform   _____ persuade

2. Jordan gazed out the starship's port. There was nothing to be seen. No stars. No nebulae. No distant galaxies. Nothing. So this was what a black hole looked like close-up, he thought. Two minutes elapsed. Only six more to go. Then he would know. Either he'd be torn apart by the terrible gravity, or he'd pop through into a white hole and come out in another universe. He took a deep breath, crossed his fingers, and waited.

    _____ entertain   _____ inform   _____ persuade

ACTIVITY 86 **Compare and Contrast**

Name:_____

Date:_____

Read the following, and then fill in the Venn diagram below.

   Both planets and comets are large objects orbiting the sun. Planets are much larger than comets, however. Some planets and all comets are mostly made up of ice. Comets are much smaller than planets. They have an erratic orbit that brings them near the sun only once in a very long while. Then they swing far out into space again. Planets have a stable orbit that keeps them about the same distance from the sun all of the time. When a comet's orbit is closest to the sun, the sun's heat begins to melt it, and solar winds blow a huge tail of gas millions of miles behind it. This tail reflects the sunlight and can be seen by us for a few days or weeks. That is why a comet looks like a shooting star. Planets also reflect sunlight and look like stars.

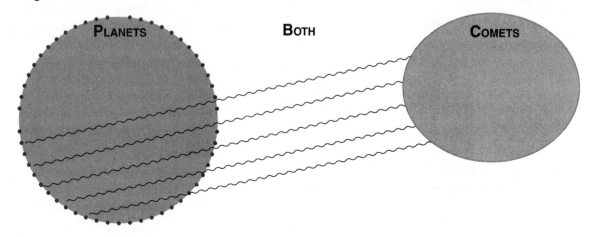

Outer Space (cont.)

ACTIVITY 87 | **Context Clues**

Name: _____

Date: _____

Read the paragraph below, and then, using the context clues, write the boldface word from the paragraph next to the word that means the same as the words below.

The stars you see at night are just a **smattering** of all the stars there are in the universe. Astronomers **estimate** that there are trillions of stars out there somewhere. Only a small **percentage** of them can be seen with the naked eye. Others can be **observed** through a telescope. Some are so **remote** that they cannot be seen at all. Stars are born and **expire** all the time. Stars come in **various** colors. Hot stars **range** in color from yellow to blue-white. Cooler stars have a more reddish **appearance**.

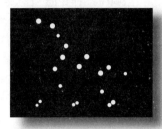

1. seen _____

2. little bit _____

3. far away _____

4. look _____

5. different _____

6. guess _____

7. die _____

8. vary _____

9. fraction _____

ACTIVITY 88 | **Cause and Effect**

Name: _____

Date: _____

Read the following paragraph. Then, for each pair of sentences below, write a "C" if the sentence is a cause; write "E" if the sentence is an effect.

Nebulae are huge clouds of dust in deep space. They are also "star nurseries." Clumps of gas and dust are pulled together by their own gravity. These form dark nebulae that begin to spin. As their gravity increases, they begin to spin faster, and gas rushes to the center of the mass. This makes the center begin to get very hot. Eventually, this baby star is spinning so fast that plumes of dust and gas shoot out of it. Once the temperature in a baby star reaches 50 million degrees Fahrenheit, hydrogen atoms start fusing into helium atoms, and the star begins to shine.

_____ 1. Clouds of dust and gas in deep space get pulled together by their own gravity.
_____ 2. A dark nebulae forms.

_____ 3. The center gets very hot.
_____ 4. Gravity increases, the nebulae spin faster, and gas rushes to the center.

_____ 5. A baby star spins very fast.
_____ 6. Plumes of dust and gas shoot out of it.

_____ 7. The star begins to shine.
_____ 8. The temperature gets so hot that hydrogen atoms begin to fuse.

Outer Space (cont.)

ACTIVITY 89 Character Analysis

Name:_____

Date:_____

An astronaut spends a long time in a very small space, usually with other people. He or she has to perform difficult tasks and experiments in zero gravity. Before they get to space, astronauts spend a long time getting prepared. They have to be in top physical shape and take lots of special classes about spaceships and other complex subjects. When they are in space, they sometimes have to go outside the ship and work all alone. If something goes wrong, they have to deal with it quickly, without panic. They know when they take off that, if something really goes wrong, they won't make it back to Earth.

1. List five character traits that are important for astronauts to have. _____

   _____ _____ _____ _____

2. Do you think you'd make a good astronaut? _____

3. Why or why not? _____

   _____

ACTIVITY 90 Details

Name:_____

Date:_____

Read the following, and then, starting with the moon, list all the categories mentioned from smallest to largest object or grouping.

The more we learn about our **universe**, the more astounding it is. The largest objects we've identified are called filaments. A **filament** is a long string of superclusters. A **supercluster** is a closely (for space) bunched group of galaxies. A **galaxy** is a very large collection of stars, planets, moons, and other objects that orbit the stars, such as comets. A **star** with its orbiting **planets** and their satellites is known as a **solar system**. In our solar system, Earth is the third planet from our star, the sun. Earth has one **moon**.

1. Moon

2. _____

3. _____

4. _____

5. _____

6. _____

7. _____

8. _____

Outer Space (cont.)

ACTIVITY 91   Drawing Conclusions   Name:_____

Date:_____

Read the following paragraph, and then answer the questions below.

Since 1960, astronomers have had equipment that is powerful enough to pick up radio signals from outer space, but so far they haven't heard anything interesting. One problem is that space is so vast that the odds of tuning in to the right direction at the right time to pick up a specific signal are very small. Also, it takes a long time for any kind of signal to travel from one place to another in space. If there were people on a planet in the nearest star system, Alpha Centauri, it would take over eight years for them to say hello to you, and for you to answer back. If you tried to talk to someone even farther away, your grandchildren would be the ones to receive the answer.

1. Why do you think scientists would like to talk to someone from another planet?

   _____

2. If you could ask someone from Alpha Centauri one question, what would it be?

   _____

ACTIVITY 92   Fact and Opinion   Name:_____

Date:_____

A fact can be proved. An opinion is what you believe or think. Read the sentences below. Put "F" by the facts and "O" by the opinions.

_____ 1. The galaxy that Earth is in is called the Milky Way.

_____ 2. I think it is a good name because it looks like a streak of milk in the sky.

_____ 3. The Milky Way is a spiral galaxy.

_____ 4. The Milky Way contains about 200 billion stars and is 70,000 light-years wide.

_____ 5. I can't even imagine something as big as a galaxy.

_____ 6. The stars in the Milky Way revolve around its center like the planets revolve around the sun.

_____ 7. The other kinds of galaxies are barred spiral, elliptical, and irregular.

_____ 8. I'm glad the Milky Way is a spiral galaxy because I think it's the prettiest kind.

49

Outer Space (cont.)

ACTIVITY 93 **Following Directions**

Name:_____

Date:_____

Long ago, people would gaze at the stars and see pictures, like in a connect-the-dots book. Then, they would make up stories about the pictures. Different people made up different stories about the same stars. For example, there are seven stars that some people called the "Big Dipper" because, to them, it looked like a cup with a long handle. Other people linked those seven stars to some other stars and called them Ursa Major, or the Big Bear.

In the circle to the right, draw seven to twelve stars to make a constellation of your own. Name your constellation and, on another sheet of paper, write a story about it.

The name of my constellation is:

_____

_____

ACTIVITY 94 **Inference**

Name:_____

Date:_____

Read the following, and then answer the questions below.

"We can't get enough thrust to get the probe all the way to Jupiter," said one of the rocket scientists. "What are we going to do?"

"We could study Venus again," someone else said. "We know we can get a space probe there."

"That's true, we can," said one of the other scientists, looking thoughtful. "I wonder. Have you ever thrown a discus?"

"Can't say that I have," the first scientist replied. "What's that got to do with the probe?"

"To throw a discus, you spin around before letting go. It makes the disc go farther than if you threw it straight. What if we didn't send the probe to Venus, just near enough for it to get caught in the gravitational spin of the planet?"

"Yes! I see what you mean." The first scientist started scribbling equations on a scrap of paper. "It should work," he said, looking up after a few moments. "Let's get busy, friends. With a little help from the goddess of love, our probe is going to Jupiter!"

1.   Who is the goddess of love? _____

2.   What are the scientists planning to do? _____

_____

Outer Space (cont.)

ACTIVITY 95 **Main Idea**

Name: _____

Date: _____

Read the paragraph below, and then put a plus (+) next to the main idea.

An interesting space happening is a binary star system. **Binary stars** are two stars that are so close together they orbit around each other. If you look at the night sky, many stars that appear from Earth to be close together are really light-years apart. These are called **optical binaries** to distinguish them from true binaries. Binary stars can sometimes be seen through a telescope and are sometimes only detected by using special equipment. Some binaries orbit each other in such a way that, from our viewpoint, they eclipse each other. These are called **eclipsing binaries**. Binary stars are quite common. If Jupiter had been just a little bigger, and had become a star instead of a planet, we might be living in a binary system.

_____ 1. Optical binaries only look like they are close together.

_____ 2. Jupiter might have become a star if it was a little bigger.

_____ 3. Binary star systems are an interesting and common space occurrence.

ACTIVITY 96 **Predicting Outcomes**

Name: _____

Date: _____

The human body has evolved in a specific amount of gravity—that of Earth. Even working on a space station for an extended amount of time has caused astronauts' bodies to change shape. Scientists and science fiction writers both know about this. They guess what kind of bodies people would have after living for a long time on another planet with different gravity. Less gravity would probably make people grow taller and have lighter bones. More gravity would probably make people shorter with heavier bones.

Read the following descriptions of two planets and draw a picture in the boxes of what people from each planet might look like.

Mars is smaller than Earth and has only one-third of Earth's gravity. Because of this, Mars has a much thinner atmosphere than Earth. If people ever live on Mars, they'd probably look like this:		Jupiter is the largest planet, with gravity two and one-half times greater than Earth's. Because of this and the poisonous cloud cover, people will probably never live on Jupiter. If they did, though, they'd look like this:	

Outer Space (cont.)

ACTIVITY 97 Sequencing

Name:_____

Date:_____

The "Race for Space" between the Soviet Union and the United States was big news in the 1960s. Yuri Gagarin was the first man to orbit the Earth in 1961. John Glenn was the second, in 1962, going around three times to Gagarin's single orbit. In 1963, Valentina Tereshkova was the first woman astronaut. She orbited the Earth 48 times. In 1965, Alexei Lionov made the first space walk. Also in 1965, Walter Schirra and Thomas Stafford made the first rendezvous of two ships in space. Finally, in 1969, Neil Armstrong and Edwin (Buzz) Aldrin, Jr., were the first astronauts to walk on the moon.

List the name and date of each space milestone on the list below. Write "S" for Soviet Union and "U" for United States after each entry.

	Name	**Date**	**S or U**
1.	First Earth orbit _____	_____	_____
2.	Second Earth orbit _____	_____	_____
3.	First woman in space _____	_____	_____
4.	First space walk _____	_____	_____
5.	First rendezvous _____	_____	_____
6.	First moon walk _____	_____	_____

ACTIVITY 98 Summarizing

Name:_____

Date:_____

Read the following paragraph, and then put a plus (+) next to the summarizing sentence.

Once people looked at the night sky and made up stories of heroes and magical beasts. They knew nothing about galaxies, supernovas, or nebulae. Now, children look up and dream about visiting the moon or colonizing Mars or perhaps even going to another solar system altogether. Some of the dreams may never come to pass. On the other hand, who knows? A hundred years ago, the moon was as unreachable as the farthest galaxy. Now, there are human footprints on its dusty surface. The sky is not the limit any more!

Write a summarizing sentence. _____

_____

_____

_____

The Civil War

ACTIVITY 99 **Author's Purpose**

Name: _____

Date: _____

Read the following paragraphs. Decide if the author's purpose is to entertain, inform, or persuade. Then put a plus (+) next to the answer.

1. The United States Civil War took place from 1861 to 1865 between the Northern states, or Union, and the Southern states that seceded from the Union and formed the Confederacy. It is generally known in the South as the War Between the States and is also called the War of the Rebellion, the War of Secession, and the War for Southern Independence. It was a bitter conflict that often pitted members of the same community, and even the same family, against each other.

    _____ entertain   _____ inform   _____ persuade

2. "What sort of a war was this," Susanna wondered, "where brother fought against brother and fathers and sons did their best to kill each other?" It was a father and brother she was looking for now—hers. Word had reached them that Seth had been wounded and taken to the same army hospital where Pa was already a patient. Surely, in a hospital, it wouldn't matter what color uniform you wore. The blood was all the same shade of red. If she hurried, if they were still alive, if they could mend their differences, perhaps she could take them both home with her to Ma.

    _____ entertain   _____ inform   _____ persuade

ACTIVITY 100 **Compare and Contrast**

Name: _____

Date: _____

Read the following and answer the questions below.

Though slavery is considered the biggest issue of the Civil War, the underlying problem was the fact that life in the North and South was so different. This led to a great deal of misunderstanding and hard feelings. In the South, most of the wealth came from huge plantations. Slaves were used to cultivate and harvest the crops and were considered vital to the economy. In the North, farms were smaller. Much of the North's wealth came from industry, for which unskilled, forced labor was impractical. People in the North thought the Southern plantation owners were cruel and lazy. People in the South thought the Northern factory owners were stupid and uncouth. Many people on both sides believed that their way was the right way and were not interested in finding a compromise.

1. In what ways were the North and South the same? _____

    _____

2. In what ways were they different? _____

    _____

The Civil War (cont.)

ACTIVITY 101 **Context Clues**

Name:_____

Date:_____

Read the following excerpt from President Lincoln's 1863 Gettysburg Address. Write the words in bold in the box next to the right meaning.

Four score and seven years ago, our **forefathers** brought forth on this continent a new nation, **conceived** in liberty and dedicated to the **proposition** that all men are created equal. Now we are **engaged** in a great civil war, testing whether that nation, or any nation, so conceived and so dedicated can long **endure**. We are met on a great battlefield of that war. We have come to dedicate a **portion** of that field as a final resting place for those who here gave their lives that this nation might live.

1. begun

2. idea

3. caught up in

4. part

5. ancestors

6. survive

ACTIVITY 102 **Cause and Effect**

Name:_____

Date:_____

Fill in the blanks with the cause or effect.

At the time of the Civil War, doctors, or surgeons as they were called, got very little training. Many wounded soldiers were dying from lack of proper medical care. A "field manual" was written in 1863 by J.J. Chisholm, a Confederate surgeon. It was very useful for both Confederate and Union doctors. The minié balls used in the guns of the time shattered bones and carried bacteria and infection into the wounds. Because of this, about three out of every four operations were amputations. When the amputation was completed, the surgeon would sew up the arteries and veins with silk thread if they were in the North, and cotton thread if they were in the South.

1. _____, many soldiers were dying from lack of care.

2. J.J. Chisholm wrote a medical "field manual." _____.

3. _____, about three of four operations were amputations.

4. Because silk was easier to get in the North, _____.

5. _____, Southern surgeons used cotton to sew wounds.

The Civil War (cont.)

ACTIVITY 103 Character Analysis

Name:_____

Date:_____

Dorothea Dix was the Superintendent of Female Nurses for the Union during the Civil War. She was called Dragon Dix because she didn't back down in an argument. Many men were convinced that women shouldn't be in the field hospitals. Dix showed them they were wrong. There were 2,000 nurses under Dix during the war. She looked after the welfare of both her nurses and the soldiers they took care of. If she couldn't get supplies from the government, she would keep looking until she found private donors. Many men owed their lives to the work of Dix and her nurses.

Think of five character traits that describe Dorothea Dix.

_____   _____

_____   _____

_____

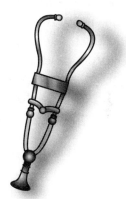

ACTIVITY 104 Details

Name:_____

Date:_____

There were no radios or televisions in the 1860s. People didn't pay for sound bites to get their message out. Instead, they made up slogans, made speeches, and sang songs that got people excited about certain ideas and taking certain actions.

Read the following stanzas from two popular Civil War songs, and then answer the questions below.

DIXIE	LIBERTY BALL
I wish I was in the land of cotton,	Come all ye true friends of the nation,
Old times there are not forgotten;	Attend to humanity's call;
Look away! Look away! Look away, Dixie Land!	Come aid in the slaves' liberation,
Oh, I wish I was in Dixie, away, away	And roll on the Liberty Ball
In Dixie Land I'll take my stand	And roll on the Liberty Ball
To live and die in Dixie.	And roll on the Liberty Ball.

1. Which song was sung in the North? _____

2. Which detail(s) tell you this? _____

3. Which song was sung in the South? _____

4. Which detail(s) tell you this? _____

The Civil War (cont.)

ACTIVITY 105 Drawing Conclusions

Name: _____

Date: _____

Read the following paragraph, and then answer the questions that follow.

Long before the Civil War, tensions were rising. People in the South were angry because they didn't think the government should control their right to own slaves. People in the North were angry because they didn't think the government should allow slavery to continue. In 1850, California wanted to become a state. People argued about whether it should be a Southern state that allowed slavery or a Northern state that didn't. To try and smooth things over, the Compromise of 1850 was drawn up. To make the Northern states happy, the Compromise stated that California would come into the Union as a free state. To make the Southern states happy, the Compromise included the Fugitive Slave Act, which made it illegal to help an escaping slave, even in the North. There was a big problem with this compromise, however. What was it?

Write your conclusion here. _____

_____

_____

ACTIVITY 106 Fact and Opinion

Name: _____

Date: _____

A fact can be proved. An opinion is what you believe or think. Read the sentences below. Put "F" by the facts and "O" by the opinions.

_____ 1. Abraham Lincoln was the president during the Civil War.

_____ 2. I think he was the best president the United States ever had.

_____ 3. Mr. Lincoln probably did everything he could to prevent a war.

_____ 4. If more people had listened to him, I believe the Civil War would never have

happened.

_____ 5. In the end, he could not keep the Southern states from seceding.

_____ 6. Once that happened, war was inevitable.

_____ 7. I imagine the day the Civil War started was the most terrible day of Abraham

Lincoln's life.

The Civil War (cont.)

ACTIVITY 107 **Following Directions**

Name: _____

Date: _____

After the Civil War, many soldiers, especially ones who had been maimed, had no way to earn a living. Some of them sold "clothes-peg dolls." These dolls were painted and dressed up to look like Civil War figures. Often, their clothes were made out of scraps of old uniforms. Find a picture of a soldier, nurse, or other person from the Civil War era. Cut out the clothes-peg outline below. Use markers, paints, or fabric scraps to dress it in a period outfit.

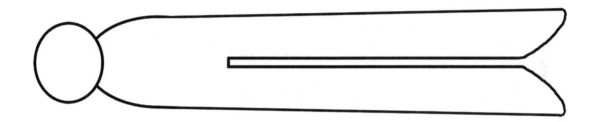

Bonus Project: Make a class diorama of a Civil War scene using your clothes-peg people.

- -

ACTIVITY 108 **Inference**

Name: _____

Date: _____

Read the following paragraph, and then answer the questions below.

Annabelle brushed the dirt off her skirt as best she could. It dragged in the mud because she didn't have a hoop to hold it out. Everything had gone to the war effort, even the steel in her hoop skirt. She started digging again. The soldiers had trampled all the crops above the ground, but maybe there were a few turnips left that she could find for the children. She thought of the old days when she'd had beautiful dresses and lots of food, and others did the digging and the water hauling and all the other chores she hadn't even known existed. Well, that was then, and this was now. Time to get back and start cooking dinner. Surely the war couldn't go on forever. The army was in tatters, and so was the land. What was the point of fighting any more?

1. Do you think this scene takes place in the North or South? _____

2. Who is Annabelle? _____

    _____

3. Why didn't she know anything about doing chores? _____

    _____

The Civil War (cont.)

ACTIVITY 109 **Main Idea**

Name:_____

Date:_____

Read the paragraph below, and then put a plus (+) next to the main idea.

The movie *Gone With the Wind* was based on the well-known fictional character, Scarlett O'Hara, who gets caught up in the war and the destruction it caused in the South. The movie shows how much the Civil War affected everybody, not just the soldiers who fought in it. *Gone With the Wind* is a love story, but it is also a war story. If you want to get a real feel for what it was like to live through the Civil War, watch this movie.

_____ 1. Scarlett O'Hara is a well-known fictional character.

_____ 2. *Gone With the Wind* shows what it was like to live through the Civil War.

_____ 3. *Gone With the Wind* is a love story set during the Civil War.

ACTIVITY 110 **Predicting Outcomes**

Name:_____

Date:_____

Read the following paragraph, and then answer the questions below.

When the Southern states seceded from the Union, most European countries assumed they would win their independence. They thought that history was on the side of the underdog. The United Netherlands had successfully seceded from Spain. Greece had seceded from the Turkish Empire. The American Colonies successfully revolted against England. However, the South lost the war, so the Union was preserved. What if the South had won? How would things have been different?

1. There are three countries on the North American continent. How many would there be if the South had won? _____ Why? _____

_____

2. Do you think slavery would still be legal in the South if they had won the war?_____ Why or why not? _____

_____

3. What do you think would have been the biggest difference in America today if the South had won? _____

_____

The Civil War (cont.)

ACTIVITY 111   **Sequencing**

Name: _____

Date: _____

The following sentences tell about Clara Barton, a famous Civil War figure. However, they are all scrambled up. Number the sentences in the proper sequence from 1 to 8.

Clara Barton was born in 1821.

_____ a.   Clara went to Andersonville and marked the graves of the men on the list.

_____ b.   People began writing to Barton, begging her to find their missing family members.

_____ c.   Barton tracked down 22,000 missing soldiers between 1865 and 1868.

_____ d.   During the Civil War, Clara Barton was one of many field nurses known as "Angels of the Battlefield."

_____ e.   She was the first woman to head a government bureau, the "Missing Soldiers Office."

_____ f.   She also published the list of the dead soldiers' names so people would know what had happened to their loved ones and where they were buried.

_____ g.   After the war, a former war prisoner brought Barton a list of 13,000 Union prisoners who had died at Andersonville.

_____ h.   Not all of the soldiers she found were happy to be located, as they had disappeared on purpose to avoid debts or other problems.

ACTIVITY 112   **Summarizing**

Name: _____

Date: _____

Read the following paragraph, and then write a summarizing sentence on the lines below.

The Civil War had many long-lasting results. It is the only war since the American Revolution in which American soldiers fought on American soil. It took the South, where much of the fighting occurred, a long time to recover. It drastically changed the population by killing more Americans than any other war the United States has ever been involved in. Though slavery ceased, and the Union continued, the war left a rift that is still not fully healed. Of all the wars Americans have fought, the Civil War is the one that has had the greatest effect on the nation.

Write a summarizing sentence. _____

_____

_____

_____

The Land Down Under

ACTIVITY 113 **Author's Purpose**

Name:_____

Date:_____

Read the following paragraphs. Decide if the author's purpose is to entertain, inform, or persuade. Then put a plus (+) next to the answer.

1. Australia is the sixth-largest country in the world and the only one that is also a continent. It is nearly as big as the continental United States. However, it only has nineteen million people, about two-thirds of the population of California. Australians are proud of their country and welcome tourists and visitors to their country.

    _____ entertain   _____ inform   _____ persuade

2. G'day, Mate! Next time you're planning a vacation, why not try Australia? It's not nearly as crowded as the United States, but it's just as big. There are beaches, cities, mountains, deserts, jungles, and grassy plains. Whatever you want we've got. No worries. Come to Australia and find out what's up in the "Land Down Under."

    _____ entertain   _____ inform   _____ persuade

ACTIVITY 114 **Compare and Contrast**

Name:_____

Date:_____

Read the following paragraph and answer the questions below.

Most of the animals in Australia are **marsupials**. Two of those marsupials are wallabies and koalas. Both carry their babies around in pouches. Both have gray fur and are about the same size. Wallabies are a type of kangaroo. They stand on their hind legs and have a long, muscular tail. They are grazers, eating a variety of grasses and leaves. Koalas are tree dwellers. They have no tail to speak of, and they have two thumbs. They seldom touch the ground, and then only to get from one tree to another. They eat eucalyptus leaves and are very particular, sometimes smelling a dozen leaves before finding one they like.

1. How are wallabies and koalas similar?_____

    _____

2. How are they different?_____

    _____

3. If you could have either a wallaby or a koala for a pet, which would you prefer? _____

    Why? _____

    _____

The Land Down Under (cont.)

ACTIVITY 115 **Context Clues**

Name:_____

Date:_____

Choose a word or phrase from the Word Bank to replace the word in boldface in each sentence. Look for context clues to help you choose the right word.

WORD BANK

green middle separates dry scary mild

1. Australia is shaped like a bowl with mountains around the rim and a vast desert in the **interior**._____

2. Most Australians live along the coast where the weather is **temperate**.

   _____

3. The Great Dividing Range **isolates** the coast from the desert._____

4. The northern coast gets plenty of rain, so it is humid and **lush**._____

5. The southern part of the continent is much more flat and **arid**._____

6. Most visitors find the interior **intimidating** and stick to the cities._____

ACTIVITY 116 **Cause and Effect**

Name:_____

Date:_____

Read the paragraph, and then draw a line from the cause on the left to the effect on the right.

A very strange town in Australia is Coober Pedy. It is in the western desert, and about 75% of its buildings are underground. This is because the climate is very hot, with temperatures often as high as 120° F. The underground houses stay comfortably cool. The reason Coober Pedy exists at all is because there are opals in the area. In fact, most of the opals in the world come from around Coober Pedy. The first opals were discovered in 1915. Soldiers from World War I, who had lived in dugouts on the battlefields, made similar "digs" for themselves when they went opal prospecting. The name of the town comes from the aboriginal words *kupa piti*, which means "white men's burrow." Coober Pedy looks so strange that several science fiction movies have been filmed there.

1. It is very hot in Western Australia.
2. In 1915, opals were discovered.
3. World War I soldiers lived in dugouts.
4. There are many opals in Coober Pedy.
5. *Kupa piti* means "white men's burrow."
6. Coober Pedy looks very odd.

a. Most of the world's opals come from there.
b. This is where the town got its name.
c. Sci-fi movies have been made there.
d. Most of Coober Pedy is underground
e. The town of Coober Pedy was started.
f. They made similar shelters in Coober Pedy.

The Land Down Under (cont.)

ACTIVITY 117 **Character Analysis**

Name: _____

Date: _____

Australia was originally named New Holland, but the name was changed by an English naval officer, Mathew Flinders. He explored Botany Bay, where Sydney is now located, and sailed around Tasmania. In 1801 he was put in charge of an expedition that sailed all the way around Australia, proving that it was a continent. He suggested the name Australia from the Latin word *australis*, which means "southern." He was only forty when he died, but he had been to more places in his short lifetime than most people ever go.

1. List four character traits you think Flinders might have had. _____

   _____   _____   _____

2. If you had lived in 1801, would you like to have sailed with Flinders? _____

   Why or why not? _____

   _____

   _____

   _____

- -

ACTIVITY 118 **Details**

Name: _____

Date: _____

Read the following paragraph, and then fill in the blanks on the time line below.

Australia's Outback has very few people living in it. Ranches, called "stations" in Australia, are sometimes hundreds of miles apart. Since 1951, children in these remote places have been able to attend Schools of the Air. Schools of the Air are a branch of the Flying Doctor Service. Stations in the Outback have shortwave radios to keep in contact with each other and to signal for help. Station children use radios, telephones, and the Internet to take lessons from a teacher at a central base. The students form clubs, learn to play musical instruments, and talk to other students in their class, as well as working on lessons.

1. What are ranches called in Australia? _____

2. When did Schools of the Air begin? _____

3. Of what service are they a part? _____

4. Name three things Schools of the Air students do via radio.

   _____   _____   _____

5. Why are Schools of the Air necessary? _____

   _____

The Land Down Under (cont.)

ACTIVITY 119 **Drawing Conclusions**

Name: _____

Date: _____

The following verses are from the Australian song, "Waltzing Matilda," which contains some Australian slang and some aboriginal words. The slang words use English, but are not common expressions in America. Read the song and look at the list of words at the bottom of the page. Write "SL" if you think it is a slang word. Write "AB" if you think it is an aboriginal word. Then, put the letter of the definition next to its corresponding Australian word.

Waltzing Matilda

Once a jolly swagman camped by a billabong
Under the shade of a coolibah tree
And he sang as he watched and waited 'til his billy boiled
You'll come a-waltzing Matilda with me!

Down came a jumbuck to drink at the water hole
Up jumped the swagman and grabbed him with glee
And he sang as he stowed the jumbuck in his tucker bag
You'll come a-waltzing Matilda with me!

_____ 1. swagman _____
_____ 2. coolibah tree _____
_____ 3. billabong _____
_____ 4. billy _____
_____ 5. jumbuck _____
_____ 6. tucker bag _____
_____ 7. glee _____

a. sheep
b. water hole
c. food sack
d. happiness
e. tramp
f. kettle
g. eucalyptus tree

ACTIVITY 120 **Fact and Opinion**

Name: _____

Date: _____

A fact can be proved. An opinion is what you believe or think. Read the sentences below. Put "F" by the facts and "O" by the opinions.

_____ 1. The people who lived in Australia when it was discovered by white explorers are called aborigines.

_____ 2. Aborigines were hunters and gatherers, not farmers.

_____ 3. I don't think I could survive in the Australian desert.

_____ 4. The aborigines ate whatever they caught or found.

_____ 5. Emu steaks and roast witchey grubs are two aboriginal foods that are now being served in some Australian restaurants.

_____ 6. Kangaroo-tail soup sounds like a strange dish to me.

_____ 7. An aboriginal child would probably think our food is weird, too.

The Land Down Under (cont.)

ACTIVITY 121 **Following Directions**   Name:_____

Date:_____

Aboriginal bark paintings are very beautiful. They are stylized pictures of the animals, plants, and mythic figures of the Dreamtime, the place the aborigines believe they come from at birth, return to at death, and visit in their dreams and visions. To make your own bark painting, take a piece of brown construction paper. Using a black marker, make an outline of one or more real or imagined animal on your paper. Add dots of white, red, blue, and yellow paint, inside and outside of the outline, filling in the shapes and giving them a magical look.

Bonus Project*:* Collect all of the paintings into a class book.

ACTIVITY 122 **Inference**   Name:_____

Date:_____

Read the following, and then answer the questions below.

"Hey, mate, want to play football?" Collin asked.

"Football? Sure!" Kevin said. "I used to play all the time back home. I was the quarterback last season."

"Good on ya! Here, catch," said Collin, tossing a ball to Kevin.

Kevin looked at it. It didn't look like the footballs he was used to. He shrugged. He was getting used to things being a little strange—like ordering a burger and getting a slice of beet on it instead of tomato.

They went out into a big field with a large circle marked on it. Four posts were evenly spaced at one side of the field. Kevin looked at them and sighed.

"Collin," he said, throwing the football back to his friend. "You'd better explain the rules to me before we start to play."

1. What nationality do you think Kevin is? _____

2. What nationality do you think Collin is? _____

3. Where do you think this story takes place? _____

The Land Down Under (cont.)

ACTIVITY 123 Main Idea

Name:_____

Date:_____

Read the paragraph below, and then put a plus (+) next to the main idea.

One of the hardest things for someone from the Northern Hemisphere to get used to about Australia is the fact that the seasons are reversed. That means holidays that are celebrated in the winter up north are summer holidays for Australians. For example, many Aussies have a beach party or a barbecue for Christmas and New Year's. Of course, it's just as hard for someone from Australia to go to America or Europe and have their holidays topsy-turvy. If only the Earth's axis were straight up and down, we'd all have the same weather and seasons—and wouldn't that be boring?

_____ 1. It's confusing but interesting to have seasons reversed in Australia.

_____ 2. Australians usually have a barbecue on Christmas.

_____ 3. If the earth's axis were straight up and down, we wouldn't have holidays.

ACTIVITY 124 Predicting Outcomes

Name:_____

Date:_____

Read the following experiment, and put a plus (+) next to the most likely outcome.

One of the interesting features of Australia is its fences. The famous Australian Dingo Fence is the longest manmade object on the planet, over twice as long as the Great Wall of China. Both the Dingo Fence and the shorter Rabbit-Proof Fence were put up to try and control the problems of dingos attacking the sheep herds and rabbits destroying grazing lands. The fences are maintained by fence riders, who repair breaks in the fences and also spread poisons along them.

_____ 1. Australia's dingos and rabbits will stay where they belong.

_____ 2. The fences will only be partly successful in keeping the dingos and rabbits

where they belong.

_____ 3. Fence riders will demand more pay for their work.

65

The Land Down Under (cont.)

ACTIVITY 125 Sequencing

Name: _____

Date: _____

Australian aborigines don't have a calendar divided by months. Instead, they keep track of time by seasons. Each season is linked to both the weather and the kind of food available. In the western desert, there are five seasons: Manggala—wet, lots of food of all sorts; Marul—end of the rainy season, nuts and mangrove pods ripen; Pargan—cold winds, honey and fish; Wilburu—hot southeast winds, goanna lizard hunting; Ladja— very hot and dry, kangaroo hunting.

Number the seasons below from 1 to 5. Draw a line from the season on the left to the matching weather and food on the right.

_____ a.	Pargan	wet, all sorts of food
_____ b.	Manggala	hot and dry, kangaroo
_____ c.	Marul	hot southeast winds, goanna lizard
_____ d.	Ladja	end of the rainy season, nuts and mangrove pods
_____ e.	Wilburu	cold winds, honey and fish

ACTIVITY 126 Summarizing

Name: _____

Date: _____

Read the following paragraph, and then write a summarizing sentence.

The vast inland desert of Australia is known as the "Outback." Though most white Australians live in the coastal cities, and many have never been very far inland, the Outback is part of the identity of every Aussie. They may not pay attention to it, but they always know it is there. The Outback is both stark and beautiful. Many people visit it. Artists love to paint it. Miners see it as a treasure trove because of the gold, gems, and metals found there. But for the people of the Outback, the aborigines, whose ancestors have lived in the desert for many thousand years, the vast, arid center of the continent is simply home.

Write a summarizing sentence. _____

_____

_____

Sports and Athletes

ACTIVITY 127 Author's Purpose

Name:_____

Date:_____

Read the following posters. Decide if the author's purpose is to entertain, inform, or persuade. Then put a plus (+) next to the answer.

1.
> The sign-up for the
> **_Hays City Soccer League_**
> spring season will be this
> Saturday at Volunteer Park.
> Teams forming for ages 8 to 18.
> Wear suitable clothing
> and running shoes.
> Tryouts and placement will begin
> at 9:00 A.M. in front of the bleachers.

2.
> _Soccer It To Me!_
> Come to Volunteer Park this
> Saturday at 9:00 A.M. and
> try out for the new
> **_Hays City Soccer League._**
> Teams forming for all ages.
> Don't miss out on the fun!
> _See you there!_

1. _____ a. entertain
   _____ b. inform
   _____ c. persuade

2. _____ a. entertain
   _____ b. inform
   _____ c. persuade

ACTIVITY 128 Compare and Contrast

Name:_____

Date:_____

Read the following, and then fill in the Venn diagram below.

Badminton and tennis are both sports that are played with racquets and a net. However, the racquets in tennis are heavier, and the net is lower. Tennis is played with a ball, and badminton is played with a shuttlecock—a small rubber or plastic tip with feathers or plastic webbing attached. Both games can be played by two to four people. In tennis, the ball may bounce once before being hit back across the net. In badminton, the shuttlecock is supposed to stay airborne. To start either game, a server uses his or her racquet to hit the ball or shuttlecock over the net to the opposing team, which must then hit it back. If a team fails to get the ball or shuttlecock back over the net or hits it out of bounds, the other team gets a point.

BADMINTON	BOTH	TENNIS

Sports and Athletes (cont.)

ACTIVITY 129 **Context Clues**

Name: _____

Date: _____

Choose a word or phrase from the Word Bank to replace the word in boldface in each sentence. Look for context clues to help you choose the right word.

WORD BANK					
named	brought	changed	convinced	allowed	common

1. When volleyball began in Germany in 1893, it was **designated** *faustball.*

   _____

2. In *faustball,* it was **permissible** for the ball to bounce before being hit back.

   _____

3. William Morgan, a YMCA coach, **imported** the game to the U.S. _____

4. He **altered** the rules by adding "no bouncing" and renamed it *mintonette.*

   _____

5. The director of the YMCA **persuaded** him to change the name to "volleyball."

   _____

6. Volleyball is now a **widespread** and popular sport. _____

ACTIVITY 130 **Cause and Effect**

Name: _____

Date: _____

Read the paragraph, and then fill in the cause or effect.

Mark Spitz was a very fine swimmer. In 1968, when he was eighteen, he won a place on the U.S. Olympic swim team. Before he went, he boasted that he would win six gold medals. However, he won only two, both for relay races. This made Mark determined to do better next time. The Olympics only take place once every four years, which gave him plenty of time to train and get stronger. Mark worked very hard for the next four years. In 1972, Mark competed in seven events. He won the gold medal in all seven events. He also set a new world record in every event. Because he did such an amazing thing, Mark Spitz is a great example of how hard work can really pay off.

THE GREATEST

Cause	Effect
1. _____	He went to the 1968 Olympics.
2. He only won two gold medals that year.	_____
3. _____,	so he had plenty of time to train.
4. Mark worked very hard.	_____
5. _____,	Mark Spitz is a great example to others.

Sports and Athletes (cont.)

ACTIVITY 131 **Character Analysis**

Name:_____

Date:_____

Gail Devers was a track star who won an Olympic gold medal in 1992. This was an amazing feat considering that she had battled a serious pre-cancerous thyroid condition that was treated with radiation. Although the radiation halted the disease, it also burned her feet so badly that the doctors recommended they be amputated. Gail refused. She had been a runner before her illness. She began training again as soon as she was able to get back on her feet. This was in March of 1991. She began running races and qualified for the U.S. Olympic track team that summer. In 1992, she went to Barcelona and won the women's 100-yard dash.

1. List three character traits that Gail Devers had.

   _____   _____   _____

2. What's the most difficult challenge you've ever faced? _____

   _____

3. What did you do? _____

   _____

Bonus Activity: Exchange answers with another person in your class and discuss.

- -

ACTIVITY 132 **Details**

Name:_____

Date:_____

Archery, the art of shooting an arrow from a bow, has been around for thousands of years and was used by ancient people in every part of the world except Australia. The phrase "firing a parting shot" was originally a Parthian shot. Parthia was an ancient empire in the Middle East. Parthians were both great archers and great horsemen. Parthian warriors would turn in the saddle and fire at the enemy as they rode past. They seldom missed. When firearms became common, archery was no longer used for warfare. However, many people still practice archery as a sport. Whether you shoot a bow on the left or right side of your body depends on which of your eyes is dominant. Generally, your dominant eye is opposite from your dominant hand. It takes a keen eye, strong arms, and a steady hand to be a good archer.

1. If you are left-handed, which of your eyes is probably dominant?

   _____

2. The ancient people on what continent did not have archery? _____

3. What replaced archery in warfare? _____

4. What is the origin of the phrase "a parting shot"?_____

5. What three things do you need to be a good archer?

   _____   _____   _____

Sports and Athletes (cont.)

ACTIVITY 133 **Drawing Conclusions**   Name:_____

Date:_____

Boxing as a sport goes back to the Greeks. Romans preferred to watch the more brutal gladiator contests, and boxing fell out of favor until seventeenth-century England. At that time, gentlemen would frequent boxing salons. Gentleman Jackson was both a professional boxer and owner of a famous salon during the Regency period in the early ninteenth century. The style of boxing at this time was bare knuckle. Because fists are hard and bony, this was very dangerous. Men were often badly injured or killed during a bare-knuckle match.

In the 1880s, a change took place in boxing. Based on what you read above and what you know about this sport now, what do you think this change was?

_____

_____

_____

ACTIVITY 134 **Fact and Opinion**   Name:_____

Date:_____

A fact can be proved. An opinion is what you believe or think. Read the sentences below. Put "F" by the facts and "O" by the opinions.

_____ 1. *Glima* is a special kind of wrestling done in Iceland.

_____ 2. The word *glima* is often translated as "game of joy."

_____ 3. It may also be associated with the word "glimmer" because *glima* wrestlers move so quickly.

_____ 4. *Glima* has a code of honor that calls for fairness and respect.

_____ 5. In *glima* wrestling, opponents always stand up and can only move clockwise around each other.

_____ 6. Learning *glima* sounds difficult, but it can be a lot of fun.

Sports and Athletes (cont.)

ACTIVITY 135 **Following Directions**

Name:_____

Date:_____

Thumb wrestling is an easy sport to play. Follow these directions to have your own thumb wrestling game.

1. Opponents sit facing each other across a table.

2. Each rests his or her right elbow on the table.

3. Opponents lock fingertips with each other.

4. Keep thumbs up.

5. Count "one, two, three" and begin.

6. The object of the game is to trap your opponent's thumb under your own.

7. The first person who either gets his or her thumb trapped or lets go is the loser.

Bonus Activity: Have a thumb wrestling championship in your class.

ACTIVITY 136 **Inference**

Name:_____

Date:_____

Read the following, and then put a plus (+) next to the right answers.

It was the last game of the 1961 season. Roger Maris ground his heel into the plate and gave his bat a test swing. This was it. He had tied the Babe's record of 60 in a single season. One more, just one. That's all he wanted. The pitcher went into his windup, leaned back, and let the ball fly. Roger stepped forward and gave it all he had. "Crack!" The bat connected solidly with the baseball and sent it soaring into the outfield—no, beyond the outfield. The crowd went crazy as Roger trotted around the bases, waving his cap. He'd done it. He'd broken a record that had been unbeatable for over thirty years. His name would go down in history.

1. The game Roger Maris played is:

_____ a. cricket.

_____ b. bowling.

_____ c. baseball.

2. The record Roger Maris broke is for:

_____ a. home runs in a season.

_____ b. runs batted in.

_____ c. lifetime batting average.

3. "The Babe" referred to is:

_____ a. Baby Face Nelson.

_____ b. Babe Ruth.

_____ c. Barbra Streisand.

Sports and Athletes (cont.)

ACTIVITY 137 **Main Idea**

Name:_____

Date:_____

Read the paragraph below, and then put a plus (+) next to the main idea.

Miniature golf was invented in 1867 at the Ladies' Putting Club of St. Andrews, Scotland. At the time, it was considered unladylike for a woman to swing a golf club past her shoulder. So a miniature version of regular golf was adapted for women to play. The game became very popular in the 1910s and 1920s. It was called "garden golf" and played on grass. The miniature golf courses on which families now enjoy playing today, with rubberized fairways, moving windmills, and whimsical hazards has come a long way from a lady's gentle pastime.

_____ 1. Miniature golf used to be played on grass.

_____ 2. Miniature golf began as a ladies' sport, but developed into a family game.

_____ 3. Women in 1867 never behaved in unladylike ways.

ACTIVITY 138 **Predicting Outcomes**

Name:_____

Date:_____

Read the paragraph below, and then put a plus (+) next to its most likely outcome.

The All-American Girls' Professional Baseball League began during World War II. The league was formed because so many male baseball players were away fighting in the war. Baseball promoters wanted the sport to continue to be in the public eye, which meant that someone had to keep playing it professionally, and the only "someones" available were girls. At first, there were many differences between women's and men's baseball, including the size of the diamond, the pitching styles, and the size of the ball. Gradually, the women's rules changed until the two games were nearly identical. After the war ended, the men's leagues started up again. In general, women who had taken on men's roles during the war were expected to give up their places to the returning soldiers.

_____ 1. The men's and women's leagues began playing against each other.

_____ 2. People continued to come to the women's games and ignored the men.

_____ 3. The women's league gradually lost its fans and was phased out by the mid-1950s.

Sports and Athletes (cont.)

ACTIVITY 139 **Sequencing**   Name: _____

Date: _____

Below are the rules for Australian Rules Football. However, they are out of sequence. Number them in proper order from 1 to 7.

_____ a. There is no standard size for the field, but it is usually about 200 feet long.

_____ b. Both teams try to get the ball down to the end of the field and through the posts.

_____ c. "Aussie Rules" is played with a ball that is a little larger than an American football, and with rounder ends.

_____ d. The game is played on a round or oval playing field.

_____ e. If the ball goes between one of the center posts and a side post, the team scores 1 point.

_____ f. There are four goal posts spaced seven yards apart at one end of the field.

_____ g. If the ball goes between the center posts, the team scores 6 points.

ACTIVITY 140 **Summarizing**   Name: _____

Date: _____

Read the following paragraph, and then write a summarizing sentence for it.

In every sport, there are athletes whose performance is head and shoulders above the rest. These men and women become heroes to many people. Of course, not all athletes are so heroic off the playing field. Some, however, take their position as a role model seriously and volunteer for many organizations and good causes. They know their name will bring whatever they do to the attention of a lot of people. From visiting children's hospitals to raising money for literacy programs, athlete celebrities have done a lot of good in many places for many people around the world.

Write a summarizing sentence. _____

_____

_____

_____

Just for Fun

ACTIVITY 141 **Author's Purpose**

Name: _____

Date: _____

Read the following paragraphs. Decide if the author's purpose is to entertain, inform, or persuade. Then put a plus (+) next to the answer.

1. How would you like to be as strong as a superhero? Mightygro Vitamins can help. Just take two Mightygro Vitamins a day, eat lots of good food, exercise, and get plenty of sleep. You'll be amazed at how great you'll feel and how strong you'll be. Mightygro: The vitamins Superman wishes he had. Don't delay, try some today!

   _____ entertain   _____ inform   _____ persuade

2. Audrey saw an ad for Mightygro. "If two Mightygros make me strong, the whole bottle will make me super-strong," she decided. She took the whole bottle. It made her super-sick. "I'm never going to believe ads again," Audrey declared. The next day, she saw an ad for Superlox. It said a spoonful of Superlox a day would make your hair thick and shiny. Audrey got a bottle of Superlox and drank it all. The next day even her tongue had hair growing on it. Some people never learn!

   _____ entertain   _____ inform   _____ persuade

Activity 142 **Compare and Contrast**

Name: _____

Date: _____

Read the following, and then fill in the Venn diagram below.

Clowns and mimes are a lot alike. Both wear makeup. Both must be very good athletes. Both go through rigorous training. Clowns, however, are usually colorfully dressed and do lots of "sight gags," such as pulling a rubber chicken out of their pants or taking "pratfalls." Clowns may or may not speak. Mimes are always silent. They dress only in black and white, and they have a much more graceful way of moving than clowns. Mimes can look like they are climbing a rope or walking, without actually going anywhere. One well-known mime act is behaving as though he or she is stuck in a glass box.

CLOWNS	BOTH	MIMES

Just for Fun (cont.)

ACTIVITY 143 Context Clues

Name: _____

Date: _____

Choose a word or phrase from the Word Bank to replace the word in bold in each sentence. Look for context clues to help you choose the right word.

WORD BANK					
making	collect	many kinds	fancy	strange	make

1. People enjoy all sorts of **unusual** hobbies. _____

2. Some people **accumulate** string and wind it into huge balls. _____

3. I read about a person who makes **elaborate** sculptures out of gum.

   _____

4. Some people **fashion** purses and other accessories out of duct tape.

   _____

5. One man got so good at **fabricating** Lego sculptures, that he quit his job and is a professional Lego model maker. _____

6. Many people collect a **variety** of objects, from stamps to antique autos, for a hobby. _____

ACTIVITY 144 Cause and Effect

Name: _____

Date: _____

Many famous toys began as other things. Look at the list of causes on the left. What toy do think developed from each cause? Write each toy in the corresponding box.

1. Egyptian children make hoops out of grapevines and twirl them around their waists.

2. College students at Yale throw tin pie plates from the Frisbie pie company to each other through the air.

3. A teacher in the 1700s glues a map of Europe to thin wood and cuts it apart with a jigsaw for his students to reassemble.

4. A company that makes wax crayons for building construction starts adding colors to the wax and sells them to teachers.

5. A naval engineer drops a big spring when he's working on a ship's engine and is fascinated by the way it flops around.

6. A teacher's brother gives her some of the doughy stuff that his company uses to clean wallpaper, and she gives it to her students to play with.

Just for Fun (cont.)

ACTIVITY 145 **Character Analysis**   Name:_____

Date:_____

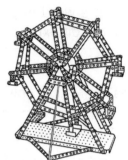

The Erector set and many other toys were invented by a man named A.C. Gilbert. By the time he died in 1962, Mr. Gilbert had 150 patents, mostly for things to do with the toys he created. He wanted his toys to be educational as well as fun. In addition to the Erector set, his company made model trains, a glass-blowing kit, and various chemistry sets. He had great respect for children's intelligence and their ability to understand science. His toys were not just "child's play."

1.   List five words that describe A.C. Gilbert's personality.

_____   _____   _____

_____   _____

2.   Which of Mr. Gilbert's toys do you think would be the most interesting?

_____

Why? _____

_____

ACTIVITY 146 **Details**   Name:_____

Date:_____

Read the following paragraph, and then fill in the details below.

H. Ty Warner didn't invent a better mouse trap. He invented a better stuffed animal. By using foam beads instead of fiberfill stuffing, his little animals have a floppy, cuddly feel to them. He started his toy company in 1983 with bigger animals. They sold well, but he wanted something different—something children could buy with their own allowance money. So, in 1993, he began making mini-animals that sold for under $5.00, and the Beanie Babies empire was born. Now, Mr. Warner is a multi-billionaire. He gives millions of dollars to good causes and sent 10,000 Beanie Babies to the children of Iraq.

Beanie Babies were invented in _____. In 1983, _____

began his toy company. Warner's animals were stuffed with _____

instead of fiberfill. Warner sent _____ _____

_____ to Iraq. The original Beanie Babies cost under

_____.

Just for Fun (cont.)

ACTIVITY 147 **Drawing Conclusions**   Name: _____

Date: _____

Gina wiped her hands on her thighs as she gazed nervously into the air. The big top seemed much bigger with an audience in it, she thought.

"Ready, Sis?" Nikko whispered. Gina hardly recognized him in his spangled tights.

"I-I'm not sure," she whispered back.

"What's not to be sure about? We've been rehearsing for weeks. I'll be right there to catch you, every time. I promise."

"I know, but . . . ." her voice trailed off.

"There's a first time for everything, Gina mia," her mother spoke in her ear. "You are a Flying Gallatti. You will be fine. Now go!"

Gina had no more time to argue. Their music had begun. She and Nikko ran out into the spotlight and began to climb. The moment she'd been waiting for all her life was here.

1. What are Gina and Nikko about to do? _____

2. What clues did you use to figure this out? _____

_____

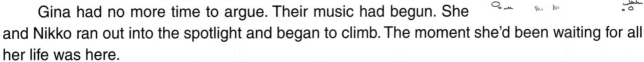

ACTIVITY 148 **Fact and Opinion**   Name: _____

Date: _____

A fact can be proved. An opinion is what you believe or think. Read the sentences below. Put "F" by the facts and "O" by the opinions.

_____ 1. I think Jim Carrey is a very funny man.

_____ 2. Not many people realize that Jim Carrey was born in Canada.

_____ 3. My favorite Jim Carrey film is *The Mask*.

_____ 4. Jim Carrey has won several Golden Globe awards.

_____ 5. Jim Carrey was paid $20,000,000 to appear in *The Cable Guy*.

_____ 6. I thought *Ace Ventura* was a lot funnier than *The Cable Guy*.

_____ 7. In *A Series of Unfortunate Events*, Jim Carrey wore many disguises.

Just for Fun (cont.)

ACTIVITY 149 **Following Directions**

Name:_____

Date:_____

Fads are silly things that are very popular for a short while and then go out of style. Pet Rocks were a fad that was very big for a while. They consisted of a small cardboard box with an ordinary rock in it and a set of directions for the "care and feeding of your Pet Rock."

Here is a set of directions for the care and feeding of a similar idea, a "Pet Stick." Read the directions and use the words from the Word Bank below to fill in the blanks.

wood	fetch	termites	indoors
matches	decorated	swelling	walking

Care and Feeding of a Pet Stick

1. Keep your pet away from _____, candles, and other sources of fire.
2. Pet Sticks cannot survive in the wild, so keep your pet _____ at all times.
3. Do not use Pet Sticks for playing _____ with your dog or other animal.
4. If your Pet Stick is injured, treat immediately with Elmer's _____ glue.
5. A larger version Pet Stick for outdoor use is the Pet _____ Stick.
6. Pet Sticks are generally housebroken. If accidents occur, check for _____.
7. When bathing Pet Sticks, some _____ may be noticed.
8. Pet Sticks can be _____ with feathers, string, and beads to make a Pet Talking Stick.

ACTIVITY 150 **Inference**

Name:_____

Date:_____

"The first thing you must learn, son, is that it is your job to make the king smile when he is feeling low."

"Why, Papa?" little Nicky asked, waving the stick his father gave him and making the bells ring.

"Our family has served the royal family in this way for generations. If there were no one to make the king laugh, it would be hard for his subjects. A sad or angry monarch takes his rage or sadness out on his people. The second thing you need to learn is how and when to speak up to the king."

"That sounds scary," Nicky stopped waving the stick and stared at his father.

"It can be, but someone must tell him unpleasant truths. We behave foolishly so that our telling doesn't sting his pride too much. Do you understand?"

"I think so," said Nicky, straightening his silly hat. "How do we begin?"

"That's my boy," said his father, "We'll start with juggling for today."

Nicky and his father are:

_____ a. mimes.   _____ b. clowns.   _____ c. jesters.

78

Just for Fun (cont.)

ACTIVITY 151 · Main Idea

Name: _____

Date: _____

Read the following paragraph, and then put a plus (+) next to the main idea.

Carnival is a word used to mean a traveling collection of amusement rides that go from town to town. Many towns have carnivals come for a week or so in the summer. It is a lot of fun to ride the merry-go-round, the ferris wheel, and the other, faster rides. Places where the rides are bigger, permanent installations are called amusement parks. Disneyland and Disney World are two very big amusement parks that most people have heard of. There are also lots of smaller amusement parks all over the United States and the world. Whether you go to a small carnival or a huge amusement park, get ready for a lot of fun!

_____ 1. Carnivals and amusement parks are both a lot of fun.

_____ 2. Carnivals move around from place to place

_____ 3. Amusement parks are permanent installations.

ACTIVITY 152 · Predicting Outcomes

Name: _____

Date: _____

"I want to go on the Tilt-a-Whirl!" said Jack as soon as they got to the amusement park.

"Oh, Jack, you always say that and then you hate it," said his big sister Paula.

"Yeah, last year you barfed all the way home," his little brother, Sam, reminded him.

"That was last year," Jack said. "I'm sure I'll be okay this time. I almost never get carsick anymore."

"Almost, huh? Okay, I'll tell you what. Let's go on some of the other rides first. If you do okay on them, you can go on the Tilt-a-Whirl. Deal?" said Paula.

"Deal!" said Jack. He shook his fist at the Tilt-a-Whirl. "This time you won't make me sick, you old ride, you!"

What do you predict will happen when Jack rides the Tilt-a-Whirl?

_____

_____

Just for Fun (cont.)

ACTIVITY 153 Sequencing

Name:_____

Date:_____

Juggling has been around for at least 4,000 years. Tomb paintings in Egypt dating back to about 2000 B.C. have been found. In a 770 B.C. scroll, a Chinese juggler, Lan Zi, is described as juggling seven swords to impress his enemies. A Greek statue from about 300 B.C. shows a man with balls balanced on his arms. Around A.D. 50, a Roman named Tagatus Ursus had carved on his tombstone that he was the first person to juggle with glass balls. There is a story from around A.D. 400 about the Irish hero Cuchulainn juggling nine apples. During the Middle Ages, from about A.D. 500 to A.D. 1500, juggling was frowned upon, and jugglers, called "gleemen" were considered low class. It got more popular again, and in A.D. 1680, the first juggling school was opened in Germany. Now jugglers are considered accomplished athletes and juggle everything from balls to knives to fire.

Put the correct date with each sentence below.

_____ 1. Cuchulainn juggles nine apples.

_____ 2. Lan Zi juggles swords to impress his enemies.

_____ 3. Jugglers were shown on Egyptian tomb paintings.

_____ 4. Tagatus Ursus' tombstone says he is the first person to juggle glass balls.

_____ 5. Jugglers are called "gleemen" and are considered low class.

_____ 6. The first juggling school opens in Germany.

_____ 7. A Greek statue is made of a man balancing balls on his arms.

ACTIVITY 154 Summarizing

Name:_____

Date:_____

Read the following paragraph, and then write a summarizing sentence.

A well-known proverb says that "a merry heart doeth good like a medicine." This may be truer than even the proverb writer realized. Scientists have discovered that laughter and other positive emotions trigger the release of endorphins into the bloodstream. Endorphins decrease pain and relieve stress. Norman Cousins wrote a book about using laughter to help him heal from a serious illness. Patch Adams, a well-known doctor, wears a clown nose and has established a clinic where laughter is a part of every patient's treatment. So be sure to get your recommended daily dose of laughter today. Your body will thank you.

Write a summarizing sentence. _____

_____

_____

_____

Taking Action

ACTIVITY 155 Author's Purpose

Name:_____

Date:_____

Read the following paragraphs. Decide if the author's purpose is to entertain, inform, or persuade. Then put a plus (+) next to the answer.

1.   Geordie took one last look around the campsite. No trash, no cans. They'd even put the sod back over the spot where they'd made their campfire.

"Ready to go, Buddy?" his dad asked, stowing his coffee cup in his backpack.

Geordie sighed. "I guess so," he said. "I'm sure going to miss being here."

"Me, too," replied his dad. "This has been a great hiking trip. But this is the last day of your school break, so we'd better get back to civilization."

_____ entertain   _____ inform   _____ persuade

2.   Originally, wildlife refuges were set aside as places where animals were not to be hunted. However, the overpopulation of some animals has created problems with disease. Also, these animals can be the cause of vehicle accidents. In order to balance the overpopulation situation, game animals are hunted in protected areas.

_____ entertain   _____ inform   _____ persuade

ACTIVITY 156 Compare and Contrast

Name:_____

Date:_____

Read the following labels for two kinds of bathroom cleaners, and then answer the questions below.

**FRIENDS OF THE EARTH
SHOWER CLEANER**

CAUTION: Mild eye irritant. In case of accidental eye contact, flush with water. Consult a physician if irritation persists.

**MISTER BUBBLY
BATHROOM CLEANER**

WARNING: Causes substantial but temporary eye injury. Do not get in eyes or on clothes. Wear protective eyewear (goggles, face shield, or safety glasses.) If eye contact occurs, call Poison Control.

1.   What do both products have in common? _____

2.   How are the two products different? _____

3.   Which product would you rather use? _____

Taking Action (cont.)

ACTIVITY 157 **Context Clues**

Name:_____

Date:_____

Choose a word or phrase from the Word Bank to replace the word in boldface in each sentence. Look for context clues to help you choose the right word.

WORD BANK						
stop	deadly	located	many	thrown away	asked	agreed

1. When Jessie Lyman was 9 years old, she helped **ban** the use of Styrofoam containers in her hometown. _____

2. Jessie lived in Freeport, Maine, which is **situated** on the Atlantic coast. _____

3. She and her friends were concerned that fast-food containers were being **discarded** in the ocean. _____

4. Styrofoam looks like food to fish and other wildlife, but it is **lethal** to them. _____

5. Jessie and her friends **implored** the town council to outlaw Styrofoam. _____

6. The town council **acquiesced** to their request and banned Styrofoam use. _____

7. The story of Jessie and her friends is just one of **numerous** stories about kids making a difference. _____

ACTIVITY 158 **Cause and Effect**

Name:_____

Date:_____

Everyone can make a difference, right in their own neighborhood. Is there trash on the streets? Get together with some friends and pick it up. Are there homeless people in your town? Donate some clothes and toys to the homeless shelter. If you like animals, volunteer at your local humane society one Saturday a month. Start a food drive for families in your area who are struggling to make ends meet. Do you know a single mom who could use a break? Offer to babysit for her sometime. If you like books, volunteer at the local library. Look around. There are lots of causes out there upon which you could have a positive effect.

Write down a cause in your town or neighborhood and what you intend to do about it.

_____

_____

_____

_____

_____

Taking Action (cont.)

ACTIVITY 159 Character Analysis

Name:_____

Date:_____

Andrew and Simon both want to earn some money. Andrew has a hard time getting up in the morning. He likes computer games, reading, and making model cars and airplanes, especially doing the painting and other detail work. He is always on time. Except for riding his bicycle, he doesn't care much for exercise or sports.

Simon jumps out of bed in the morning, raring to go. He likes computer games too, but doesn't have much time for them because he's usually too busy playing soccer or baseball. Actually, he likes any kind of sports. He's smart and gets good grades, but almost never reads anything outside of school work.

Read the ads below. Which boy would be best suited for each job?

1. Name: _____

Help Wanted: Bicycle paper carrier. Early morning route. Must be able to carry heavy bag of papers while peddling and have good throwing arm. Call George at: 555-1234.

2. Name: _____

Help Wanted: Bookshop helper. I need someone to come in two or three afternoons a week to stock shelves and sweep up. Must be punctual and detail oriented. Fill out application at: Trumble's Book Store, 123 Main Street.

ACTIVITY 160 Details

Name:_____

Date:_____

Read the selection, and then put a plus (+) next to the correct answers.

"Let's do something different for Valentine's Day," Sam suggested to the class in early February. "Instead of giving store-bought valentines to each other, let's make valentines for everybody at the nursing home where my mother works."

The class thought this was a really thoughtful idea. Each student brought in some supplies. George got lace doilies in red, white, and gold. Sabrina collected all her mother's seed catalogs so they could use the flower pictures. Allison brought red and pink construction paper. Darren contributed glitter glue. They worked on the valentines for a little while every afternoon the week before Valentine's Day.

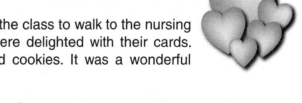

On Valentine's Day, Mrs. Allen got permission for the class to walk to the nursing home and deliver the valentines. The people there were delighted with their cards. Sam's mother surprised the students with punch and cookies. It was a wonderful Valentine's Day for everybody.

1. The students decided to make valentines for the people at the nursing home because:
   - _____ a. it would get them out of school.
   - _____ b. they were bored.
   - _____ c. it was a nice thing to do.

2. Sabrina brought seed catalogs because:
   - _____ a. they could use the flower pictures to make valentines.
   - _____ b. it was getting close to spring.
   - _____ c. Mrs. Allen wanted to order seeds for the class.

Taking Action (cont.)

ACTIVITY 161 **Drawing Conclusions**

Name:_____

Date:_____

Dumb animals may not be so dumb after all. Chimpanzees are not able to speak, but they can be taught to use sign language. One chimpanzee, named Washoe, even made up her own words, such as "drink-fruit" for watermelon and "hurt cry food" for radishes. When she was given an adopted chimpanzee son, she taught him over seventy words. Gorillas have learned sign language too. Many scientists believe dolphins and whales have a language they converse in. Some dogs learn complicated commands, and even cats come when they are called—if they feel like it.

1. Think of another example of animal-to-animal or animal-to-human communications.

    _____

2. If you have a pet, do you talk to it? _____ Why or why not? _____

    _____

    _____

ACTIVITY 162 **Fact and Opinion**

Name:_____

Date:_____

A fact can be proved. An opinion is what you believe or think. Read the sentences below. Put "F" by the facts and "O" by the opinions.

_____ 1. A girl named Mary Beth Sweetland saved a duck whose beak was caught in a plastic six-pack holder.

_____ 2. It took two weeks for her to get the duck to trust her.

_____ 3. It must have been hard to see the duck suffering and not be able to help it.

_____ 4. Finally, she was able to get close enough to cut the plastic loose.

_____ 5. I think knowing you've saved an animal's life must be a great feeling.

_____ 6. When the duck flew away, Mary Beth sat down and cried for joy.

Taking Action (cont.)

ACTIVITY 163 **Following Directions**

Name: _____

Date: _____

One person's trash is another's art material. To make a recycle collage, follow the directions below.

1. Collect interesting-looking pieces of cardboard, plastic lids, buttons, scraps of fabric, etc.
2. Look around your yard or neighborhood for interesting leaves, grasses, and other natural objects.
3. Find a large, clean cardboard box and cut one side out of it.
4. Use craft or hot glue to make a background of recycled objects in the cardboard box.
5. Add detail with smaller objects, leaves, etc.
6. Give your art a title and glue a can top to the back for a hanger.
7. As an alternative, use tin cans, plastic containers, etc., to make a sculpture.

ACTIVITY 164 **Inference**

Name: _____

Date: _____

Read the following paragraph. Read each question, and then put a plus (+) next to the answer.

"We've been studying energy all week," Rajid told his mother. "Ms. Brown was glad when I told her we hang our laundry out to dry and have a vegetable garden."

"Did you mention that we only use fluorescent bulbs and just got a low-energy refrigerator too?" his mother asked.

"No, I forgot," Rajid said. "We discussed buying food locally, though, which we do. Amy mentioned that her family recycles all kinds of things, just like us. And John's father rides a bicycle to work. I said Papa always takes the bus. Everybody was surprised at how much we were all doing."

"Yes," his mother said. "If everyone does a little, it adds up to a lot."

1. What are Rajid and his mother discussing?
   _____ a. saving time
   _____ b. saving energy
   _____ c. saving money

2. Why is it good to buy local food?
   _____ a. It's fresher.
   _____ b. It uses less fuel to transport it.
   _____ c. Both of the above

3. Why is it good that John's father rides a bike to work?
   _____ a. He doesn't use the gas to drive.
   _____ b. He stays healthier.
   _____ c. Both of the above

Taking Action (cont.)

ACTIVITY 165 Main Idea

Name: _____

Date: _____

Read the paragraph below, and then put a plus (+) next to the main idea.

Charlie, Hailee, and Latasha were walking to school through the park one morning.

"Just look at this park!" exclaimed Charlie. "There is so much litter on the ground. I wish people would use the trash cans."

"Yeah, the merry-go-round and teeter-totters need some paint, too," declared Hailee.

"I have an idea," said Latasha excitedly. "Let's ask Mrs. Garcia if we could make this a class project to fix up the park and playground."

"That's an awesome idea," exclaimed Charlie. "Let's go talk to Mrs. Garcia right now!"

_____ 1. The park's playground is a fun place.

_____ 2. The students want to make the park and playground more attractive.

_____ 3. Charlie, Hailee, and Latasha are good friends.

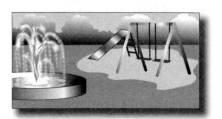

ACTIVITY 166 Predicting Outcomes

Name: _____

Date: _____

"You need to slow down, Matt," cautioned his younger brother, Jack, as they sped through an elementary school zone.

"We're running late," Matt said. "I still have to drop you off at your school and then drive to my high school."

"Well, a police officer came to talk to our class about obeying laws," explained Jack. "She said that if you don't slow down in a school zone and get ticketed, you will be fined $300. The law is for the safety of the children going to school and the crossing guards, too. Sometimes, children don't always cross at the corner, and they run out into the street in front of the cars. One could run out in front of you, and you might not be able to stop."

"I'm not going to hit anyone!" exclaimed Matt. "I'm a careful driver. I haven't gotten a ticket yet, have I?"

Just then, Matt and Jack saw some flashing lights ...

What do you think the outcome will be? (This is based on a true story, by the way.)

_____

_____

_____

Taking Action (cont.)

ACTIVITY 167 **Sequencing**

Name: _____

Date: _____

It is much easier to recycle aluminum than it is to get new aluminum from ore. You get a can of soda and drink it. Then, you smash the can and toss it into a recycling bin. It is hauled to the recycling plant. There, it is shredded into small pieces. The pieces are melted in a furnace. At this point, the recycled aluminum can't be distinguished from newly smelted aluminum. The molten aluminum is poured into molds to make ingots. The ingots are cooled. Once cooled, they are forced through big rollers to make sheets of aluminum in whatever thickness is needed.

Number the steps for recycling aluminum below from 1 to 8.

_____ a. The molten aluminum is poured into molds to make ingots.

_____ b. It is shredded into small pieces.

_____ c. You get a can of soda and drink it.

_____ d. The ingots are cooled.

_____ e. You smash the can and toss it into a recycling bin.

_____ f. The ingots are forced through big rollers.

_____ g. It is hauled to the recycling plant.

_____ h. The pieces are melted in a furnace.

ACTIVITY 168 **Summarizing**

Name: _____

Date: _____

Read the following paragraph, and then write a summarizing sentence.

In the 1960s, there was a popular saying, "You're either part of the solution or you're part of the problem." This means that everyone has the choice to just go along with things as they are or to make a difference. A lot of people choose to be part of the solution. They recycle trash to save the world's resources. They help out in churches, soup kitchens, and hospitals and work for world peace and an end to hunger. They collect food and clothes and medical supplies for disaster victims. They take in homeless people and stray animals. They volunteer at libraries and veterinarian clinics and hospices. A lot of them are children who don't want to wait until they are grown to be part of the solution. They have found a way to be effective now.

Write a summarizing sentence. _____

_____

_____

_____

Answer Keys

Activity 1: Author's Purpose (p. 4)
1. entertain   2. inform

Activity 2: Compare and Contrast (p. 4)
Squid: 10 tentacles, leaves eggs, 200 ft. long
Octopus: 8 tentacles, watches eggs, 50 ft. long
Both: cephalopods, beaks, eggs, suckers

Activity 3: Context Clues (p. 5)
1. approximately, crust, submerged, irregularity
2. dwells, perfectly, millennia, concerning

Activity 4: Cause and Effect (p. 5)
1. Eels are living batteries.
2. All creatures emit some electricity.
3. The pits are electrical sensors.
4. The eel senses an energy field.
5. A big eel gives off 600 volts of electricity.

Activity 5: Character Analysis (p. 6)
brave, curious, patient, caring, intelligent, determined

Activity 6: Details (p. 6)
1. condensation
2. precipitation   3. river
4. delta   5. ocean/sea
6. evaporation

Activity 7: Drawing Conclusions (p. 7)
1. a baby seal
2. a
3. The ocean water is dark at night.

Activity 8: Fact and Opinion (p. 7)
1. O   2. F   3. F   4. O
5. F   6. F   7. O

Activity 10: Inference (p. 8)
1. Hawaii. Answers may vary. Accept any tropical location.
2. the names, surfing, waves, palm trees, paradise
3. surfing

4. She thought it was a shark.
5. a dolphin
6. Answers will vary.

Activity 11: Main Idea (p. 9)
2. Global Positioning System technology has changed…

Activity 12: Predicting Outcomes (p. 9)
Answers will vary.

Activity 13: Sequencing (p. 10)
1. pouch   2. incubator
3. their father   4. mouth
5. leaves   6. cycle

Activity 14: Summarizing (p. 10)
Answers will vary.

Activity 15: Author's Purpose (p. 11)
1. inform   2. entertain

Activity 16: Compare and Contrast (p. 11)
Both: in Asia, similar cultures, Buddhism, silk, pictographs, population density
China: Confusianism, larger, Pop. 1 bil.
Japan: island, Zen, pop. 150 mil.

Activity 17: Context Clues (p. 12)
1. sources   2. specific
3. native   4. about
5. required   6. made

Activity 18: Cause and Effect (p. 12)
1. Because of WWII,
2. The government wanted to preserve cultural heritage.
3. Certain persons were called BIICAs.
4. They are called Living National Treasures.
5. Whenever an LNT is recognized,

Activity 19: Character Analysis (p. 13)
1.–2. Answers will vary.

Activity 20: Details (p. 13)
1. 1,400 years   2. 4,000
3. northern   4. tourist
5. seven wonders

Activity 21: Drawing Conclusions (p. 14)
b. Kite Fighting

Activity 22: Fact and Opinion (p. 14)
1. F   2. F   3. O   4. F
5. F   6. O   7. F

Activity 23: Following Directions (p. 15)
Answers will vary.

Activity 24: Inference (p. 15)
The four dragons became the four great rivers of China. Answers will vary.

Activity 25: Main Idea (p. 16)
1. China has a very long history.

Activity 26: Predicting Outcomes (p. 16)
The father found his daughter in the woods and sent the stepmother away. Answers will vary.

Activity 27: Sequencing (p. 17)

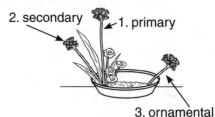

2. secondary   1. primary
3. ornamental

Activity 28: Summarizing (p. 17)
Education in China is considered a privilege that must be earned. Answers will vary.

Activity 29: Author's Purpose (p. 18)
1. inform   2. entertain

Activity 30: Compare and Contrast (p. 18)
1. Similar: They start the same, are by the same poet, and have the same meter and rhythm.
2. Different: One is hopeful, the other is depressed.
3. Answers will vary.

Activity 31: Context Clues (p. 19)
bushes
grasshopper
singer
whisper
hushed
softly singing

Activity 32: Cause and Effect (p. 19)
1. fall in love with the first person they see.
2. for Demetrius to fall in love with Helena.
3. Lysander's Helena
4. fall asleep
5. Lysander's, Demetrius'
6. the right person.

Activity 33: Character Analysis (p. 20)
1. No, his language
2. c
3. Answers will vary.

Activity 34: Details (p. 20)
1. Colonel Pickering
2. Freddy
3. Henry Higgins
4. to speak proper English
5. to work in a flower shop

Activity 35: Drawing Conclusions (p. 21)
1. the dead
2. their coffins
3. because time doesn't exist for the dead

Activity 36: Fact and Opinion (p. 21)
1. O 2. F 3. F 4. O
5. O 6. F

Activity 37: Following Directions (p. 22)
Answers will vary.

Activity 38: Inference (p. 22)
1. They find out he wasn't the real Inspector General.
2. They find out that the real Inspector General has just arrived. Answers will vary.

Activity 39: Main Idea (p. 23)
c. Plays and make believe…

Activity 40: Predicting Outcomes (p. 23)
The servant is really the prince. He and Camilla fall in love, and the spell is broken. Answers will vary.

Activity 41: Sequencing (p. 24)
a. 3 b. 1 c. 4 d. 2

Activity 42: Summarizing (p. 24)
Answers will vary.

Activity 43: Author's Purpose (p. 25)
1. entertain 2. persuade

Activity 44: Compare and Contrast (p. 25)
Cumulus: fluffy, short life, thunder-heads
Nimbus: layered, long life, soaking rain
Both: formed of water drops, same altitude

Activity 45: Context Clues (p. 26)
1. a. yearly 2. b. effects
3. a. noteworthy
4. c. happened 5. c. guess

Activity 46: Cause and Effect (p. 26)
1. E 2. C 3. E 4. C
5. E 5. C 7. C 8. E

Activity 47: Character Analysis (p. 27)
1. a laundress
2. warm, caring, motherly
3. Answers will vary.

Activity 48: Details (p. 27)
1. South Dakota and Nebraska
2. Ohio, Pennsylvania, West Virginia
3. Yes; North Dakota, Montana, Wyoming/Idaho
4. Yes; Illinois and Missouri
5. Arizona, New Mexico, Texas, Kansas, Missouri, Illinois, Indiana, Michigan

Activity 49: Drawing Conclusions (p. 28)
1. a 2. c 3. a 4. c

Activity 50: Fact and Opinion (p. 28)
1. F 2. F 3. O 4. F
5. O 6. F 7. O

Activity 52: Inference (p. 29)
1. the Midwest
   This is where tornadoes are most likely.
2. a tornado
3. They all get in the cellar, and the tornado hits.

Activity 53: Main Idea (p. 30)
1. People have been predicting…

Activity 54: Predicting Outcomes (p. 30)
1. a. wet and warm
2. c. dry and hot
3. a. wet and cold

Activity 55: Sequencing (p. 31)
a. 2 b. 5 c. 1 d. 6
e. 7 f. 3 g. 4 h. 8

Activity 56: Summarizing (p. 31)
Answers will vary.

Activity 57: Author's Purpose (p. 32)
1. persuade 2. inform

Activity 58: Compare and Contrast (p. 32)
Fajitas: onions, peppers
Burrito: refried beans, lettuce, cheese
Both: tortillas, tomatoes, chicken, salsa

Activity 59: Context Clues (p. 33)
1. needs 2. invented
3. unusual 4. poisonous
5. mystery

Activity 60: Cause and Effect (p. 33)
1. e 2. a 3. b 4. f
5. d 6. g 7. c

Activity 61: Character Analysis (p. 34)
Answers will vary. Should reflect the fact that Salizar is more demanding and Raul is willing to share.

Activity 62: Details (p. 34)
1. pigments 2. antioxidants
3. vitamins 4. nutrients
5. Complex 6. carbs
7. apple

Activity 63: Drawing Conclusions (p. 35)
1. pumpkins
2. Halloween
3. carving jack-o'-lanterns

Activity 64: Fact and Opinion (p. 35)
1. O 2. F 3. F 4. F
5. O 6. F 7. O

Activity 65: Following Directions (p. 36)
Peel; strips
tablespoons; 1
salt
cookie sheet
400; 15
10; once; 5

Activity 66: Inference (p. 36)
1. salad
2. peaches, baking chocolate, meatloaf

Activity 67: Main Idea (p. 37)
1. Eating well is better…

Activity 68: Predicting Outcomes (p. 37)
1. Tracy   2. Tracy   3. Tracy
4.–6.   Answers will vary.

Activity 69: Sequencing (p. 38)
Schedules may vary slightly.

7:10	brush teeth
7:20	water
8:10	water
10:00	morning break
10:15	water
11:50	water
12:40	water
2:30	afternoon break
4:10	water
5:00	piano practice
5:50	water
6:40	water
7:00	homework
8:00	watch TV
9:50	brush teeth

Activity 70: Summarizing (p. 38)
Answers will vary.

Activity 71: Author's Purpose (p. 39)
1. b. inform   2. c. persuade

Activity 72: Compare and Contrast (p. 39)
Ares: Hera, war, armor, spear, owls, woodpeckers, vultures
Hermes: Maia, messengers, winged helmet and sandals, staff, roosters, tortoises
Both: Zeus' sons, Greek gods

Activity 73: Context Clues (p. 40)
1. thrived   2. worshipped
3. came out   4. thought to be
5. dressed   6. gave

Activity 74: Cause and Effect (p. 40)
1. c   2. d   3. e   4. b
5. a

Activity 75: Character Analysis (p. 41)
Answers will vary.
He got too close to the Earth and died.

Activity 76: Details (p. 41)
1. e   2. d   3. h   4. i
5. c   6. a   7. b   8. g
9. f

Activity 77: Drawing Conclusions (p. 42)
The seasons

Activity 78: Fact and Opinion (p. 42)
1. F   2. O   3. F   4. F
5. O   6. F   7. O   8. F

Activity 79: Following Directions (p. 43)
Answers will vary.

Activity 80: Inference (p. 43)
1. dolphins
2. The king knew the true story and made the sailors give back the things they stole.

Activity 81: Main Idea (p. 44)
3. Many words and sayings have…

Activity 82: Predicting Outcomes (p. 44)
1. He sent Jason for the Golden Fleece.
2. Answers will vary.

Activity 83: Sequencing (p. 45)
1. d. The Nemean Lion
2. g. The Lernaean Hydra
3. j. The Hind of Ceryneia
4. a. The Erymanthean Boar
5. c. The Augean Stables
6. b. The Stymphalian Birds
7. h. The Cretan Bull
8. k. The Wild Mares of Diomedes
9. e. The Belt of Hippolyta
10. l. Geryon's Cattle

11. i. The Apples of the Hesperides
12. f. Cerberus

Activity 84: Summarizing (p. 45)
Answers will vary.

Activity 85: Author's Purpose (p. 46)
1. inform   2. entertain

Activity 86: Compare and Contrast (p. 46)
Planets: regular orbit, larger
Comets: erratic orbit, glowing tail
Both: orbit sun, look like stars

Activity 87: Context Clues (p. 47)
1. observed   2. smattering
3. remote   4. appearance
5. various   6. estimate
7. expire   8. range
9. percentage

Activity 88: Cause and Effect (p. 47)
1. C   2. E   3. E   4. C
5. C   6. E   7. E   8. C

Activity 89: Character Analysis (p. 48)
Answers will vary.

Activity 90: Details (p. 48)
1. moon   2. planet
3. sun or star   4. solar system
5. galaxy   6. supercluster
7. filament   8. universe

Activity 91: Drawing Conclusions (p. 49)
Answers will vary.

Activity 92: Fact and Opinion (p. 49)
1. F   2. O   3. F   4. F
5. O   6. F   7. F   8. O

Activity 94: Inference (p. 50)
1. Venus
2. Send the probe around Venus, and use the planet's spin to help it get to Jupiter.

Activity 95: Main Idea (p. 51)
3. Binary star systems…

Activity 96: Predicting Outcomes (p. 51)
Mars: tall and skinny
Jupiter: short and solid looking

Activity 97: Sequencing (p. 52)

Yuri Gagarin	1961	S
John Glenn	1962	U
Valentina Tereshkova	1963	S
Alexei Lionov	1965	S
Schirra and Stafford	1965	U
Armstrong and Aldrin	1969	U

Activity 98: Summarizing (p. 52)
Answers will vary.

Activity 99: Author's Purpose (p. 53)
1. inform   2. entertain

Activity 100: Compare and Contrast (p. 53)
1. Same: Both thought they were right.
2. Different: South, plantations, slavery; North, industry, slave labor not practical

Activity 101: Context Clues (p. 54)
1. conceived   2. proposition
3. engaged   4. portion
5. forefathers   6. endure

Activity 102: Cause and Effect (p. 54)
1. Because doctors weren't well trained
2. It was used by doctors on both sides.
3. Because of the use of minié balls
4. It was used to sew wounds.
5. Because cotton was plentiful in the South

Activity 103: Character Analysis (p. 55)
Answers will vary.

Activity 104: Details (p. 55)
1. Liberty Ball
2. slaves' liberation
3. Dixie
4. land of cotton

Activity 105: Drawing Conclusions (p. 56)
Neither the North nor the South were happy with it.

Activity 106: Fact and Opinion (p. 56)
1. F   2. O   3. O   4. O
5. F   6. F   7. O

Activity 108: Inference (p. 57)
1. the South
2. a Southern lady
3. The slaves did all the chores.

Activity 109: Main Idea (p. 58)
2. *Gone With the Wind* shows what…

Activity 110: Predicting Outcomes (p. 58)
1. 4; Because the Confederacy would be a separate country
2.–3. Answers will vary.

Activity 111: Sequencing (p. 59)
a. 3   b. 5   c. 7   d. 1
e. 6   f. 4   g. 2   h. 8

Activity 112: Summarizing (p. 59)
Answers will vary.

Activity 113: Author's Purpose (p. 60)
1. inform   2. persuade

Activity 114: Compare and Contrast (p. 60)
1. Similar: gray fur, marsupials, same size
2. Different: Wallabies are grazers, have long tails, live on the ground. Koalas have short tails, live in trees, eat only eucalyptus leaves
3. Answers will vary.

Activity 115: Context Clues (p. 61)
1. middle   2. mild
3. separates   4. green
5. dry   6. scary

Activity 116: Cause and Effect (p. 61)
1. d   2. e   3. f   4. a
5. b   6. c

Activity 117: Character Analysis (p. 62)
Answers will vary.

Activity 118: Details (p. 62)
1. stations
2. 1951
3. Flying Doctor Service
4. form clubs, learn music, talk to other students
5. Stations are so far away from each other.

Activity 119: Drawing Conclusions (p. 63)

1. SL, e   2. AB, g   3. AB, b
4. SL, f   5. AB, a   6. SL, c
7. SL, d

Activity 120: Fact and Opinion (p. 63)
1. F   2. F   3. O   4. F
5. F   6. O   7. O

Activity 122: Inference (p. 64)
1. American   2. Australian
3. Australia

Activity 123: Main Idea (p. 65)
1. It's confusing but interesting…

Activity 124: Predicting Outcomes (p. 65)
2. The fences will only be partly successful…

Activity 125: Sequencing (p. 66)

3	a.	Pargan	cold winds, honey and fish
1	b.	Manggala	wet, all sorts of food
2	c.	Marul	end of rainy season, nuts and mangrove pods
5	d.	Ladja	hot and dry, kangaroo
4	e.	Wilburu	hot southeast winds, goanna lizard

Activity 126: Summarizing (p. 66)
Answers will vary.

Activity 127: Author's Purpose (p. 67)
1. inform   2. persuade

Activity 128: Compare and Contrast (p. 67)
Tennis: ball, bigger racquet, low net, bounce
Badminton: shuttlecock, smaller racquet, high net, no bounce
Both: racquets, nets, 2 to 4 players

Activity 129: Context Clues (p. 68)
1. named   2. allowed
3. brought   4. changed
5. convinced   6. common

Activity 130: Cause and Effect (p. 68)
1. Mark Spitz was a great swimmer.
2. It made him more determined to win.
3. The Olympics happen every 4 years
4. He won seven gold medals
5. Since he did such an amazing thing,

Activity 131: Character Analysis (p. 69)
Answers will vary.

Activity 132: Details (p. 69)
1. right   2. Australia
3. firearms   4. Parthian shot
5. keen eye, strong arm, steady hand

Activity 133: Drawing Conclusions (p. 70)
They started using padded gloves.

Activity 134: Fact and Opinion (p. 70)
1. F   2. F   3. O   4. F
5. F   6. O

Activity 136: Inference (p. 71)
1. c   2. a   3. b

Activity 137: Main Idea (p. 72)
2. Miniature golf began…

Activity 138: Predicting Outcomes (p. 72)
The women's league gradually lost…

Activity 139: Sequencing (p. 73)
a. 2   b. 5   c. 4   d. 1
e. 7   f. 3   g. 6

Activity 140: Summarizing (p. 73)
Answers will vary.

Activity 141: Author's Purpose (p. 74)
1. persuade   2. entertain

Activity 142: Compare and Contrast (p. 74)
Clowns: colorful, pratfalls, may talk, sight gags
Mimes: black and white, silent, graceful, glass box
Both: makeup, athletes, rigorous training

Activity 143: Context Clues (p. 75)
1. strange   2. collect
3. fancy   4. make
5. making   6. many kinds

Activity 144: Cause and Effect (p. 75)
1. Hula hoops   2. Frisbees
3. Jigsaw puzzles
4. Crayola crayons
5. Slinky   6. Play Doh

Activity 145: Character Analysis (p. 76)
Answers will vary.

Activity 146: Details (p. 76)
1993
H. Ty Warner
foam beads
10,000 Beanie Babies
$5.00

Activity 147: Drawing Conclusions (p. 77)
1. a trapeze act
2. Flying Gallatti, big top, catching

Activity 148: Fact and Opinion (p. 77)
1. O   2. F   3. O   4. F
5. F   6. O   7. F

Activity 149: Following Directions (p. 78)
1. matches   2. indoors
3. fetch   4. wood
5. walking   6. termites
7. swelling   8. decorated

Activity 150: Inference (p. 78)
c

Activity 151: Main Idea (p. 79)
1. Carnivals and amusement…

Activity 152: Predicting Outcomes (p. 79)
Answers will vary.

Activity 153: Sequencing (p. 80)
1. A.D. 400
2. 770 B.C.
3. 2000 B.C.
4. A.D. 50
5. A.D. 500–1500
6. A.D. 1680
7. 300 B.C.

Activity 154: Summarizing (p. 80)
Answers will vary.

Activity 155: Author's Purpose (p. 81)
1. entertain   2. inform

Activity 156: Compare and Contrast (p. 81)
1. Both are eye irritants.
2. Mister Bubbly is more toxic.
3. Friends of the Earth

Activity 157: Context Clues (p. 82)
1. stop   2. located
3. thrown away
4. deadly   5. asked
6. agreed   7. many

Activity 158: Cause and Effect (p. 82)
Answers will vary.

Activity 159: Character Analysis (p. 83)
1. Simon   2. Andrew

Activity 160: Details (p. 83)
1. c. it was a nice thing to do.
1. a. they could use the pictures to make valentines.

Activity 161: Drawing Conclusions (p. 84)
Answers will vary.

Activity 162: Fact and Opinion (p. 84)
1. F   2. F   3. O   4. F
5. O   6. F

Activity 164: Inference (p. 85)
1. b   2. c   3. c

Activity 165: Main Idea (p. 86)
2. The students want to make…

Activity 166: Predicting Outcomes (p. 86)
Jack will probably get a ticket.

Activity 167: Sequencing (p. 87)
a. 6   b. 4   c. 1   d. 7
e. 2   f. 8   g. 3   h. 5

Activity 168: Summarizing (p. 87)
Answers will vary.